The GRAND CANYON HANDBOOK

An Insider's Guide to the Park

As related by Ranger Jack

by Susan and Phil Frank

Pomegranate

SAN FRANCISCO

Published by Pomegranate Communications, Inc.
Box 6099, Rohnert Park, California 94927
www.pomegranate.com

Pomegranate Europe Ltd.
Fullbridge House, Fullbridge
Maldon, Essex CM9 4LE, England

Library of Congress Cataloging-in-Publication Data

Frank, Susan, 1948-
    The Grand Canyon handbook : an insider's guide to the park, as related by Ranger Jack / by Susan and Phil Frank.
      p. cm.
    Includes bibliographical references and index.
    ISBN 0-7649-1276-3
    1. Grand Canyon National Park (Ariz.)--Guidebooks. I. Frank, Phil. II. Title.

F788 .F756 2000
917.91'320453--dc21

                                        99-057745

Pomegranate Catalog No. A525
ISBN 0-7649-1276-3

Interior design by Shannon Lemme

Printed in USA

09 08 07 06 05 04 03 02 01 00   10 9 8 7 6 5 4 3 2 1

· Contents ·

Many visitors arrive at the Grand Canyon with precious little information about the area or what they're about to see. This was true for our family of six when we first arrived at the Grand Canyon in 1975 with our worldly possessions packed in a moving van. We arrived without reservations or overnight arrangements during one of the busiest times of the year—the week between Christmas and New Year's—never imagining that this would be our home for the next fifteen years and that our four children would all graduate from Grand Canyon High School. Like so many others, our great expectations were no match for the first glimpse of the Canyon. I still marvel at the reactions of visitors who are standing on the rim for the first time, looking as though they are gazing out on the last frontier. The Canyon continues to have this same kind of influence on people from diverse cultures around the world.

As I look back in time, I can trace how this place has grown and changed. If you wrote to the park in 1933, you would have received a 54-page booklet with maps and photos describing every aspect of your visit. The same letter written in 1999 might produce one or two brochures containing general information about the park. Each year, 70 percent of Grand Canyon visitors arrive for their first and often last visit. Other intrepid travelers return again and again to explore every inch of the area. This book is designed to help both the first time and the repeat visitor glean some insider knowledge of this amazing place.

Another change of note is in the ranks of rangers who run the park. In 1933, visitors would have taken a guided walk with one of only three ranger-naturalists, who were all permanent National Park Service employees assigned to the Grand Canyon. Evening campfire programs were special events that often featured a prominent visiting college professor who would lecture on the human and natural history of the area. Today, most of the programs are given by seasonal rangers, often called park interpreters, who can help make your trip truly special. Visitors are often surprised to learn that these employees return year after year, just for the reward of living and working in a national park. They spend many hours researching and developing interesting walks, talks, and other programs without paid vacations and other benefits associated with permanent park employees. They certainly made my tenure at the Grand Canyon easier. In appreciation for the work of these unsung heros of the National Park system, this book is dedicated to the many seasonal rangers who make the experience of visiting the Grand Canyon so worthwhile for so many.

Jack O'Brien
Cottonwood, Arizona
December 15, 1999

·Introduction·

Grand Canyon National Park and the surrounding national forests and recreational areas offer an amazing array of natural wonders, activities, accommodations, and facilities. Before you begin your adventure there, you'll probably want to ask a few questions about what to do, and when and how to do those things. This book offers you a quick and easy way of finding the answers you need. Your guide through this handbook will be Ranger Jack—who closely resembles former Ranger Jack O'Brien, who was Chief of Interpretation at Grand Canyon for many years. He's been around long enough to have heard all the questions that visitors ask, and to know the answers. We thought he would be a natural to guide you through the Canyon as only an insider can.

The question-and-answer format we use originally came from "100+ Common Visitor Questions & Answers," a document that the National Park Service Division of Interpretation at Yosemite National Park created to help park rangers and interpretive staff there get quickly oriented.

We've updated many of those questions, provided answers specific to the Grand Canyon, and added lots of others to help you learn some inside information about this magnificent park and its surroundings. We hope our book will add to your enjoyment of the Grand Canyon, whatever your interests and however long your visit.

I
Getting there

Where is the Grand Canyon?

Chiseled along 277 miles of the Colorado River in northern Arizona, Grand Canyon National Park includes more than 1.2 million acres of forests, streams, waterfalls, alpine meadows, deserts, canyons, and plateaus. It encompasses five of North America's seven life zones and three of its four deserts. More than 500 miles of hiking trails traverse the park's three geographically distinct areas: the South Rim, the North Rim, and the Inner Canyon. The mighty Colorado River provides one of the world's longest stretches of navigable white water, dividing the park's North and South Rims. The Grand Canyon's varied terrain is home to 1,500 flowering plants, 305 bird species, 75 species of mammals, 25 kinds of fish, 50 species of amphibians and reptiles, an unknown number of insects, and some of the most awesome scenery you'll ever see.

Here are some road mileage figures to Grand Canyon National Park:

Via Interstate 40 from the west:

From Williams, Arizona	59 miles
From Ash Fork, Arizona	78 miles
From Seligman, Arizona	101 miles
From Kingman, Arizona	171 miles
From Hoover Dam	242 miles
From Las Vegas, Nevada	273 miles
From Los Angeles, California	507 miles
From San Francisco, California	820 miles

Via Interstate 40 from the east:

From Flagstaff, Arizona	92 miles
From Winslow, Arizona	150 miles
From Gallup, New Mexico	280 miles
From Albuquerque, New Mexico	415 miles

From Santa Fe, New Mexico	477 miles
From Denver, Colorado	879 miles
From St. Louis, Missouri	1,499 miles

Via Interstate 17 from the south:

From Phoenix, Arizona	247 miles
From Tucson, Arizona	334 miles

Via Highway 89 from the north:

From Zion National Park	272 miles
From Bryce Canyon National Park	310 miles
From Salt Lake City, Utah	594 miles

How do we get there?

Depending upon your time and budget, you can get to the Grand Canyon by car, plane, bus, shuttle, or train.

South Rim by Car. You can enter the park at the south entrance station from State Highway 64. From Williams or Flagstaff, Highway 64 can be reached by Interstate 40. From Williams, the south entrance to the park is 50 miles on a fairly straight but hilly two-lane road that runs through a landscape of sagebrush and desert scrub, broken up by ponderosa and pinyon-juniper forests. This route offers little in the way of gas stations, campgrounds, restaurants, or other accommodations, but that doesn't deter a steady stream of auto, bus, and RV traffic. In the winter months, the road might be icy and occasionally snowpacked, so check road conditions before you leave Williams. Once you're in the park, you'll drive or shuttle on a two-lane road to the South Rim, the new Canyon View Information Plaza (which opens in fall, 2000) and Grand Canyon Village, where most of the park's facilities and services are located. Drivers should watch for elk and deer that often dart across the road as it winds through the ponderosa forests.

From Flagstaff, you can follow U.S. Highway 180 to Highway 64, and then drive another 28 miles to the park's south entrance. Highway 180 is also a two-lane road, but with many more curves and hills than the Williams route. No services are available between Flagstaff and the Highway 64 junction, but again, traffic is usually heavy. Check road conditions before you leave Flagstaff, as winter storms occasionally close the road, and icy conditions are common. This route travels along a striking volcanic landscape; be sure to keep an eye out for the Red Butte, an erosion remnant a few miles north of the Highway 180/64 junction, and Humphreys Peak, the highest point in Arizona at 12,643 feet. Two miles outside the park, the road passes through the community of Tusayan, where visitor services can be found, including lodging, camping, food, and fuel. As you drive through the ponderosa forests, watch for elk and deer that make a habit of crossing the roads suddenly.

If you're driving from the east, U.S. Highway 89 joins with State Highway 64 near Cameron, Arizona, on the Navajo Indian Reservation. You'll find gas stations and limited food services in and around Cameron, which will provide the only services or facilities until you reach Desert View 30 miles away at the east park entrance, where you'll find limited services and seasonal gas. This route follows another two-lane hilly road, with heavy traffic that takes you through desert scrub and pinyon-juniper forests. In the winter, check road conditions before you travel.

North Rim by Car. From the north, you can reach the Grand Canyon from Las Vegas and Salt Lake City along Interstate 15. You then take State Highway 389 to Fredonia, U.S. Highway 89A to Jacob Lake, and State Highway 67 to the north entrance of the park. This route runs through canyon and plateau lands and boasts such attractions as the Kaibab Paiute Indian Reservation and Pipe Spring National Monument. But there are limited services and facilities along the way.

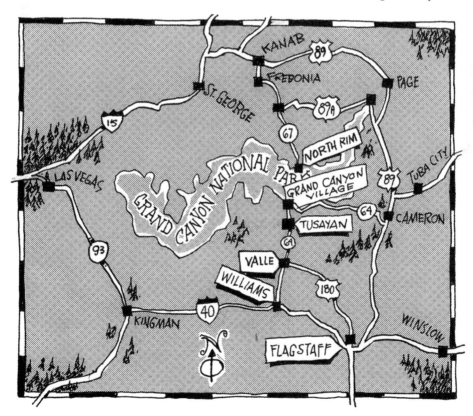

South Rim by Air. You can fly to the nearest airports at Flagstaff, Arizona (80 miles southeast); Phoenix, Arizona (220 miles south); and Las Vegas, Nevada (220 miles west). There is limited air service to the smaller Grand Canyon Airport (7 miles south of the park), with connecting shuttle service to Maswik Lodge via Cassi Tours. Call (520) 638-0821 for fare and schedule information. Major car rental agencies serve the Phoenix, Flagstaff, and Las Vegas airports. Budget Car Rental has a year-round rental desk at the Grand Canyon Airport. Call your travel agent for more information on air fares and schedules.

South Rim by Bus. Greyhound Bus Lines, (800) 231-2222, provides scheduled service to Flagstaff and Williams, Arizona from points nationwide. Service connecting to the Grand Canyon can be made through Gray Line of Flagstaff (run by Nava-Hopi Tours) at (800) 892-8687 or (520) 774-5003. For schedule and fare information, you can also check with the transportation desk at Bright Angel Lodge in the park.

South Rim by Train. AMTRAK, (800) 872-7245, provides scheduled service to Flagstaff, Arizona with connecting bus service to the Grand Canyon through Gray Line of Flagstaff (Nava-Hopi Tours). Call Gray Line at (800) 892-8687 or (520) 774-5003. The Grand Canyon Railway, (800) 843-8724, runs historic excursion trains from Williams, Arizona, to the Canyon daily (except December 24 and 25). These trains offer three classes of service departing Williams at 9:30 a.m. and arriving at the Grand Canyon at 11:45 a.m. For the return, they depart at 3:15 p.m. and arrive back in Williams at 5:30 p.m. Prices range from $51–$101 for adults, and $21–$71 for children (prices subject to change). Overnight packages are available.

North Rim by Air, Bus, Train. The nearest major cities are Salt Lake City, Utah (380 miles north), and Las Vegas, Nevada (280 miles southwest). Regularly scheduled airline, bus, and train services serve both cities. Then, you'll have to rent a car, as there is no regular air, bus, or train service directly to the North Rim.

By Transcanyon Shuttle. Daily round-trip shuttle service between the South and North Rims is provided from mid-May to mid-October. It departs North Rim at 7:00 a.m. and reaches South Rim at noon; then departs South Rim at 1:30 p.m. and arrives at North Rim at 6:30 p.m. Fare per person is $60/one-way, $100/round-trip. Call (520) 638-2820 for reservations and information.

How much does it cost to get in?

Considering that you're paying to see one of the Seven Natural Wonders of the World and one of the most beautiful and dramatic landscapes you'll ever see, it's a real bargain.

As you enter one of three park gates, you'll pay an entrance fee that's good for seven days for both Rims. A ranger will give you a map of the park with basic park information, an admission receipt, and a free copy of *The Guide*—the park newspaper with up-to-date listings and schedules for all park activities. Remember to keep your admission receipt to re-enter the park if you leave it or drive between the North and South Rims. If you're lucky enough to arrive on August 25, you won't have to pay any entrance fee, because we waive the cost on that day to honor the founding of the National Park Service. For educational fee waivers, call (520) 638-7850.

Private non-commercial vehicles $20
(valid for seven days, both Rims)

Individuals arriving by bus, foot, bicycle, horse, or skis $10
(valid for seven days, both Rims)

Annual Pass. $40
(valid for one year from date of purchase, both Rims)

Golden Eagle Pass $50
(good for all National Parks for one year from date of purchase)

Golden Age Pass $10
(a lifetime pass to all National Parks for U.S. citizens who are 62 and older)

Golden Access Pass . . . . .Free
(for blind or permanently disabled U.S. citizens or permanent residents)

When's the best time of year to see the Grand Canyon?

Speaking from experience, I can say that any season in the Grand Canyon has its rewards. It just depends on what part of the park you visit, and what you want to see and do. My favorite months are October, with its temperate weather and fewer crowds, and the often-crowded December holidays, when the Canyon may be magically clad in snow.

South Rim. The South Rim, open year-round, is the most accessible area of the park by all modes of transportation. It also has the most visitors, facilities, and services. Most visitors arrive between April and September, and the least from November through February. There is an average annual precipitation of about 16 inches. Spring usually arrives late in the high country of the South Rim (elevation 7,100 feet), with lots of unpredictable weather. March and April often combine winter and spring conditions, while May and June are traditionally the driest months. Summer arrives suddenly in June with dependably hot temperatures, large crowds, and monsoon rains in the afternoons. Summer nighttime temperatures are generally cool. Fall comes by mid-September, casting its golden light on the Canyon walls and offering temperatures that range between the high 30s (Fahrenheit) at night to the 60s during the day. You can usually expect a dusting of snow by Halloween, and a major snowstorm by Thanksgiving. Winter on the South Rim (November–February) can be very cold, with below-zero temperatures at night, and up to 60 inches of snow per year. But in any season, the weather here is erratic. Snow can fall and melt within a few days or stay on the ground all winter, or it can become a deluge of rain in December.

Inner Canyon. While ice and snow may remain on the rims, visitors who venture down below the South Rim into the Inner Canyon can enjoy the soothing desert warmth and colorful wildflowers as early as March. A mile below the North and South Rims, the Colorado River at Phantom Ranch is still 2,400 feet above sea level. Year-round, the weather here is drier and hotter than anywhere else in the park, with summer highs well over 100 degrees Fahrenheit. Rain and snow are scarce here, with a mere 7 inches of rain per year.

North Rim. This is the coolest and wettest part of the park, with about 26 inches of precipitation a year. During the visitor season, mid-May to mid-October, warm clothing and bedding are a necessity. Early in the spring at Jacob Lake, snowplows start to clear the entrance road to the park, completing the job about one month later. The North Rim opens in mid-May, usually with snow still on the ground. The rainy season runs from mid-July to mid-August, when afternoon thunderstorms may bring downpours, flash flooding, trail washouts, and lightning. As early as September the snow begins to fall, with heavy winter weather closing the North Rim to visitors in November or early December. More than 10 feet of snow will accumulate during the winter season on the North Rim.

You can enjoy any time of year at the Grand Canyon. Just keep in mind that desert and near-desert areas have no "average" seasons. Year-round, the only predictable element is the extreme and dramatic weather that makes this place one of the most scenic areas in the world.

Although the park is open 24 hours a day, 365 days a year, the roads are not. Winter snows, freezing temperatures, and dangerous driving conditions close the entrance road into the North Rim, making that area of the park unreachable by most visitors. That doesn't mean that the more adventuresome can't ski or snowshoe into the North Rim, as long as they can negotiate deep snow and cold temperatures. The state of Arizona closes the entrance road to the North Rim to vehicles on the first big snowfall, which usually occurs in early December. The entrance station closes October 15, and the Backcountry Office closes October 31. The North Rim entrance reopens to visitors in cars and buses on May 15, after the spring thaw.

Spring in the Grand Canyon often brings flash floods and rockslides that may cause certain areas of the park and hiking trails to close to visitors. On the North Rim, early spring is the time when we usually close small portions of the North Kaibab Trail for maintenance and repair from winter damage. Visitors arriving in cars can drive into the Grand Canyon Lodge, but not to Cape Royal and Point Imperial, because it takes longer to open these higher-elevation roads, which usually get more snow. In the early spring and late fall, the North Rim is usually open for day-use only. Call the North Rim Visitor Center at (520) 638-7864 for more information.

It's not always Mother Nature's fault; sometimes it's just plain human nature that makes the park inaccessible. For the first time in the park's history, the Grand Canyon was closed to visitors in 1995 and 1996, because of a government shutdown over budget negotiations.

Call (520) 638-7888 for 24-hour recorded information on park and road conditions.

What services are available?

Most of the park's visitor services are found along the South Rim of the Grand Canyon, but you'll be able to find seasonal services along the North Rim, and limited year-round services in the Inner Canyon.

South Rim. Along the South Rim and in Tusayan (just outside the south entrance) you'll find the following services:

⇨ A full range of lodging choices at the El Tovar Hotel, Kachina Lodge, Thunderbird Lodge, Bright Angel Lodge, Maswik Lodge, Yavapai Lodge, Moqui Lodge, Trailer Village, and numerous other motel lodgings (see pages 90–92 and 94–95)

⇨ Several campgrounds inside the park and in Tusaysan, including one RV campground and three backcountry campgrounds

⇨ Grand Canyon Association bookstores located in the visitor center, Yavapai Observation Station, Kolb Studio, Desert View Contact Station, and in the Tusayan Museum

⇨ Year-round and seasonal dining facilities, including the Arizona Steakhouse, dining rooms at the El Tovar Hotel and Moqui Lodge, a summer-only cookout at Moqui Lodge, a coffee shop at the Bright Angel Lodge, a snack bar at the Desert View Trading Post, and cafeterias at Maswik and Yavapai Lodges

⇨ Two general stores: one in Grand Canyon Village and one in Tusayan. These two stores, formerly Babbitt's General Stores, are now Delaware North Park Services stores. (A third store is located near the east park entrance, Desert View.) The stores will be renamed sometime in the year 2000.

- ⇨ A vast array of gift, book, and curio shops located in most lodgings, as well as in the Hopi House, Verkamp's Curios, Hermits Rest Gift Shop, Desert View Trading Post, and Lookout Studio
- ⇨ A ranger station, backcountry information center, and National Park Service administrative offices
- ⇨ A shuttle service
- ⇨ Coin-operated shower and laundry facilities next to Mather Campground
- ⇨ A medical/dental clinic and pharmacy
- ⇨ A Bank One branch office and an ATM Machine
- ⇨ A post office
- ⇨ Several churches and numerous interdenominational worship services
- ⇨ One gas station and a repair garage with towing services
- ⇨ Fax services
- ⇨ A radio station and a weekly newspaper
- ⇨ Childcare services (for park residents)
- ⇨ K–12 public schools
- ⇨ Kennels

North Rim. Visitor services on the North Rim are only available from mid-May until late October. Once overnight accommodations close for the season, there are no food, lodging, or fuel services to be found anywhere along the North Rim. During the summer and fall, the following services are available:

- ⇨ Lodging at the Grand Canyon Lodge
- ⇨ One developed campground with tent and RV sites (no hookups)
- ⇨ Shower and laundry facilities
- ⇨ A transcanyon shuttle
- ⇨ An NPS visitor center, a ranger station, and a backcountry information center
- ⇨ A Grand Canyon Association bookstore in the visitor center
- ⇨ A transportation desk
- ⇨ Dining facilities in the Grand Canyon Lodge complex, including a dining room, snack shop, saloon, and coffee bar
- ⇨ A gas station

- ➪ A grocery and general store
- ➪ A medical clinic staffed by a nurse practitioner
- ➪ A post office
- ➪ A lost-and-found office
- ➪ Interdenominational worship services

Inner Canyon. The only way to get to the Inner Canyon is by foot, mule, or horse on one of the many Canyon trails. The only lodging and meal service facility below either rim is located at Phantom Ranch near the Colorado River. The Inner Canyon has three developed campgrounds: Indian Garden below the South Rim, Bright Angel near Phantom Ranch, and Cottonwood below the North Rim. Toilets are located in several places along the trails into the canyon.

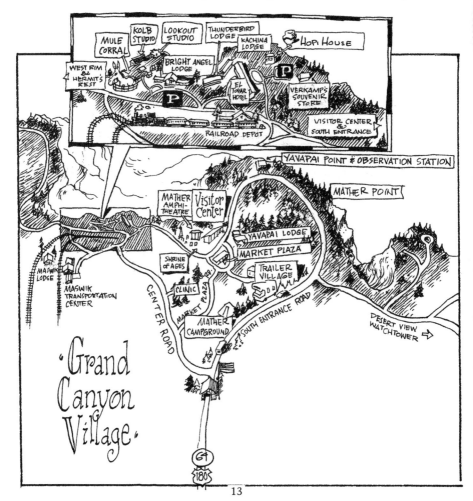

Who runs the Grand Canyon?

Although the park belongs to all of us, the United States National Park Service (NPS), which is part of the Department of the Interior, makes the rules in Grand Canyon National Park. This means you won't see any highway patrol officers, sheriffs, or municipal firefighters during your visit. Look instead for a park ranger if you need a helping hand.

The NPS has plenty of people around who make sure things run smoothly. Park rangers handle law enforcement, traffic regulation, search and rescue, and other duties. Park naturalists and interpreters (who are park rangers) provide all the educational walks, talks, and programs in the park. The people dressed in green pants, gray shirts, and dark green baseball caps are the park maintenance, fire, and resource management workers. All of us report to the NPS administrators like the superintendent and chief ranger.

The Grand Canyon Association (GCA) is a nonprofit group that operates bookstores throughout the park and publishes informational and interpretive materials in support of park programs. Supported by membership fees and donations, it also provides funds for exhibits, preservation of historic park buildings and artifacts, and development of scientific knowledge of the Grand Canyon area. Since its founding in 1932, the GCA (formerly the Grand Canyon Natural History Association) has donated nearly $8 million to the NPS. The GCA, together with the NPS, cosponsors the Grand Canyon Field Institute. This nonprofit school offers a wide range of short field courses and nature study opportunities in the park from March through November.

To help with many park services, the NPS has contracted with private concession companies, but the NPS authorizes prices and service rates. Since 1968, Amfac Parks & Resorts has operated Grand Canyon National Park Lodges and provided many park services, including lodging, food services, retail stores, service stations, interpretive sightseeing tours, and other visitor services. Delaware North Park Services operates two general stores inside the park, and Verkamp's operates the oldest gift, book, and curio store on the South Rim.

The Grand Canyon National Park Foundation is a nonprofit organization that raises money to support projects and programs approved by the NPS, including restoration, preservation, and wildlife protection in the park. The foundation is funded by corporations, foundations, and individuals interested in helping the park.

The Grand Canyon Trust is a nonprofit organization that promotes the conservation of natural resources of the Colorado Plateau. Based in Flagstaff, Arizona, the trust has successfully lobbied for regional and national legislation that helps protect the park.

You can contact the NPS, Grand Canyon concession companies, and other organizations at the following addresses or numbers:

National Park Service
P.O. Box 129
Grand Canyon, AZ 86023
(520) 638-7888
www.nps.gov
www.thecanyon.com/nps

Amfac Parks & Resorts
Grand Canyon National
  Park Lodges
P.O. Box 699
Grand Canyon, AZ 86023
(303) 29-PARKS
(520) 638-2631
www.amfac.com

Grand Canyon Association
P.O. Box 399
Grand Canyon, AZ 86023
(520) 638-2481
(800) 858-2808
www.grandcanyon.org

Grand Canyon Field Institute
P.O. Box 399
Grand Canyon, AZ 86023
(520) 638-2485
www.thecanyon.com/fieldinstitute

Delaware North Park Services
P.O. Box 159
Grand Canyon, AZ 86023
(520) 638-2262

**The Grand Canyon National
  Park Foundation**
823 N. San Francisco, Suite A
Flagstaff, AZ 86001
(520) 774-1760
www.grandcanyonfoundation.org

Grand Canyon Trust
2601 N. Fort Valley Road
Flagstaff, AZ 86001
(520) 774-7488
www.grandcanyontrust.org

What you bring depends on where you stay and what you do in the park, but I can name some basic items that will make your trip more comfortable. For advice on special activities like camping and hiking, turn to other sections of this book.

From spring through fall our weather is hard to predict. Storms can appear suddenly, bringing rain, wind, and really cold temperatures. Summers are hot and dry on the South Rim, but afternoon thunderstorms can bring sudden temperature drops. If you're in the Inner Canyon, expect scorching summer temperatures, both day and night. My advice to all visitors: be prepared for these abrupt changes. And, whatever the season, dress in layers that you can add or subtract.

The park has three distinct temperature zones. The bottom of the Inner Canyon has an elevation of about 2,400 feet, which means summertime temperatures that can exceed 110 degrees Fahrenheit. The elevation on the North Rim exceeds 9,000 feet, and on the South Rim it exceeds 7,000 feet. Expect summer temperatures on the rims to be in the 70s and 80s, with chilly nights (even in midsummer). The ultraviolet radiation is intense, so sunscreen, sunglasses, and hats are a must. The high elevation, high temperatures, and extra activity can become a problem for those visitors with breathing or heart ailments. It's best to check with your physician about special precautions you can take to help prevent heart attacks and respiratory failure.

Winter arrives quickly in the park, and if you're not prepared it can be downright dangerous. Some years our first snowfall comes in October, so don't think you'll be warm enough without a heavy parka, hiking boots with heavy socks, and thermal underwear. Heat escapes from your head and hands, so pack a pair of mittens and a warm cap that covers your ears.

You can also save yourself some worry by bringing a first-aid kit, along with a pair of boots or sturdy sneakers for hiking, bicycling, or walking. Binoculars are a must if you want to see our wildlife up close, and a camera will help you remember what you saw here. Once you're tucked away in your room, camper, or tent, it's always nice to have a good book and games to while the night away.

From late spring to fall there are nine places to stay—seven on the South Rim, one on the North Rim, and one in the Canyon—having more than 1,200 rooms and cabins. Accommodations range from basic to deluxe, and the rates vary depending upon the amenities offered. A rustic cabin without bath at the Maswik Lodge costs about $60 a night, while a luxurious suite at the El Tovar Hotel runs over $270 (based on double occupancy; all rates subject to change).

To get the best place for your needs, reserve early (six to twenty-three months in advance during peak periods) by calling Amfac Parks & Resorts at (303) 29-PARKS (297-2757). Or, you can write them at 14001 E. Iliff Avenue, Suite 600, Aurora, CO 80014. Their fax number is (303) 297-3175, or you can visit their web sites at www.amfac.com.

If you want to sleep in a tent, recreational vehicle, or under the starry sky, you can choose from five park campgrounds that you can drive to from late May to October. During the winter and early spring, this changes to four campgrounds: Mather, Trailer Village, Desert View, and Tuweep. The Desert View and Tuweep campgrounds are operated by the National Park Service on a first-come, first-served basis. Three campgrounds, Mather, North Rim, and Trailer Village, can be reserved in advance. To reserve a site at the Mather or North Rim campgrounds, call (800) 365-2267 or reserve online at http://reservations.nps.gov/. Sites at Trailer Village are reserved through Amfac Parks & Resorts at (303) 29-PARKS. Campsites go for $10–$15 a night, depending on the time of year and amenities like flush toilets and showers. You can also reserve in advance one of eighty hook-up sites (water, electric, sewer) at the Trailer Village RV campground. These sites go for about $20 a night for two people, and $1.75 for each additional person.

You can also bunk down outside the park in various lodges, hotels, motels, private campgrounds, and National Forest campgrounds. For more detailed information, turn to "Lodging and Dining," pages 94–98; or "Camping and Backpacking," pages 110–111.

Can Fido and Purr come too?

Sure. You can bring your pets as long as you follow some strict rules. Pets must be kept leashed at all times. They can go with you on paved rim trails and in the rim campgrounds, but those are the only places they can go. They can't follow you on trails below the rims, in buildings, in park buses, or in backcountry areas unless they're seeing-eye or hearing-signal dogs, or Canine Companions for people with other disabilities.

These rules are made for good reason. Our delicate ecosystem isn't ready for the wild mountain Chihuahua or the free-range Labrador. Just about any kind of pet could create problems for the park wildlife and their natural habitats, not to mention other visitors. The rules also protect your pet from possible injury or death from our summer-time heat and the narrow trails below the rims. We keep careful watch on these regulations, and we're not shy about handing out citations that can cost you up to $500.

If you bring your pet to the Canyon and want to hike below the rims, there are kennel facilities located in the South Rim Village, off Rowe Well Road, a mile south of West Rim Drive. Hours are 7:30 a.m. to 5:00 p.m. Proof of vaccinations, as well as advance reservations, are required. Call (520) 638-0534, ext. 6039 for reservations and more information. There are no kennel facilities on or near the North Rim.

III
Park Attractions

> # We only have one day to visit; what should we see and do?

Most rangers would tell you it takes several days to sample most of the wonders of the Grand Canyon, but here are a few tips for getting the most out of a single day. For current schedule and activity information, don't forget to check *The Guide* (North or South Rim editions).

SOUTH RIM (OPEN YEAR-ROUND)

You can start by getting your bearings at one of the South Rim's two visitor and information centers, located in the Grand Canyon Village and at Desert View (520/638-2736). Here you can orient yourself and learn what activities are planned in the park that day. Next, a visit to the Yavapai Observation Station (520/638-7890) will provide interesting exhibits about the fossil record in the Canyon, as well as an amazing view of the Grand Canyon from large observation windows. Don't miss the history museum and bookstore just off the lobby at the Bright Angel Lodge. You can learn more about the Canyon by viewing rotating art exhibits at the Kolb Studio (520/638-2771), or by going to the Tusayan Museum (520/638-2305) to see an 800-year-old Indian ruin and exhibit about prehistoric Pueblo life.

You can also join a ranger-led walk or talk about the geology, wildlife, and cultural resources of the Grand Canyon. These free ranger programs are offered daily and change seasonally. Some of the current progams include a sunset talk and short walk that starts from the Yavapai Observation Station an hour before sunset. Nightly in the park, you can join a ranger for an outdoor (June–September) or indoor (October–May) slide presentation about the ever-changing Grand Canyon. For more information on ranger-led activities, refer to *The Guide*, or to "Getting Around" in this book.

> On your mark... Get set...

A great way to get the large view of the Canyon is to take a free shuttle (year-round) or drive (November–April) along Hermit Road (formerly West Rim Drive). You can stop at eight viewing spots during this 16-mile, round-trip drive. Or, you can take a private vehicle or commercial bus tour along the scenic 23-mile Desert View Drive (formerly East Rim Drive). You'll see stunning canyon vistas; the Tusayan Indian Ruins; and views of the Painted Desert, Colorado River, San Francisco Peaks, and the Vermilion Cliffs from the Watchtower at Desert View. There is no better place to capture the majesty of the Grand Canyon and its surroundings than from the rims. The westernmost and easternmost points will provide the most spectacular views. Be sure to allow enough time (at least two hours for the West Rim and three hours for the East Rim) to linger at each viewpoint along the way.

If you want to slow your touring pace down, I suggest a short walk along one of the rim trails. For those who feel up to the task, a short hike into the canyon along the Bright Angel or South Kaibab Trail will provide awe-inspiring views and a memorable canyon experience. Remember to leave time for lunch at one of the restaurants along the rim before or after you trek into the canyon.

You can also buy an audio guide to the Canyon at the Village Visitor Center Bookstore for $14.95 (Travel Audios) or $9.95 (Voices of the Canyon). The programs play in your car as you drive along the rims. You'll hear park rangers tell fascinating stories about points of interest and about the geology, ecology, and wildlife of the Canyon.

NORTH RIM (MAY 15–OCTOBER 15 ONLY)
Stop at the North Rim Visitor Center which is located at the south end of the Bright Angel Point parking area. Here you'll find out everything you need to know about what to do and where to go on the North Rim. While at the visitor center, you might want to join one of the daily ranger-led programs that include walks and talks about the history, geology, flora, and fauna of the North Rim. For more information, call the visitor center at (520) 638-7864.

If you want to see the rim at your own pace you can try a variety of short- and medium-length rim walks. I would suggest the Bright Angel Point Trail, a half-mile (round trip) self-guided nature trail that begins at the log shelter at the Grand Canyon Lodge parking area. Or, you can try the three-mile (round trip) Transept Trail, which follows the rim from the Grand Canyon Lodge to the North Rim Campground and back. For those who are prepared for a longer hike, you can try the ten-mile (round trip) Uncle Jim Trail, which winds through the rim forest to Uncle Jim's Point overlooking the North Kaibab switchbacks. You can also hike the ten-mile (round trip) Widforss Trail, which has a self-guided 2.5-mile walk along the rim, then winds through the forest to Widforss Point.

Don't forget to try the dining room at the Grand Canyon Lodge, which has spectacular views of the Canyon. It's open daily during the season, serving breakfast (6:30 a.m.–10:00 a.m., and 11:00 a.m. continental); lunch (11:30 a.m.–2:30 p.m.); and dinner (5:00 p.m.–9:30 p.m.).

For those who want adventure on the back of a mule, you could try the half-day mule trips that leave daily from the Grand Canyon Lodge. You'll take a bus to the corral at 7:30 a.m., and return by 12:30 p.m. The trip descends 2,400 feet to Supai Tunnel and returns on the same route. The cost is $40, and you must be at least eight years old. Call (435) 679-8665 for more information.

These are my suggestions. Now it's up to you to design your own way of exploring this magical place. Good luck, and enjoy your day in the Grand Canyon.

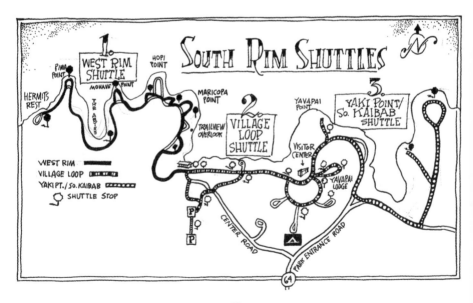

You'll probably want to stop first at one of the park visitor centers to get your bearings. Here you can talk with a ranger, view interpretive exhibits, watch a slide presentation, browse the bookstore, and pick up current information about road conditions, hiking trails, and ranger programs in the park's three main geographic areas. Then check out the other information centers listed below to learn more about the Grand Canyon.

SOUTH RIM AND INNER CANYON

South Rim Visitor Center (Grand Canyon Village): Open year-round. Six miles north of the south entrance to the park you'll find the main visitor center and park headquarters. Here you can ask questions, get oriented, and make decisions about what to do by viewing a free slide show about the Grand Canyon. It's shown every 30 minutes during visitor center hours (8:00 a.m.–5:00 p.m.). There are also exhibits about the Canyon's history, geology, wildlife, and activities, as well as a bookstore with guides, maps, and books about the park. You may want to join one of the daily ranger-led programs at the center. Depending upon the time of year, these include nature walks, fossil hunts, lectures, and evening stargazing. Check *The Guide* for current schedules and times, or call (520) 638-7888 for more information. In fall, 2000, this facility will close and a new visitor center will open at Canyon View Information Plaza.

Yavapai Observation Station (Grand Canyon Village): Open year-round. Located at Yavapai Point just three-quarters of a mile east of the visitor center, this facility offers panoramic views, exhibits, a large bookstore, and ranger-led programs. Check *The Guide* for current program schedules and times, or call (520) 638-7888.

Kolb Studio (Grand Canyon Village): Open year-round. Located at the Bright Angel Trailhead, this historic building was built in 1904 as a photography studio. It later housed a soda fountain, a small movie theater, and a gift shop. Today it offers visitors rotating art exhibits, orientation and park information, a bookstore, and ranger-led activities.

Backcountry Information Center (Maswik Transportation Center): Open year-round. Located near Maswik Lodge a few miles west of the visitor center, here's where you'll find information about camping on the rim, Inner Canyon hiking, and permits for all backcountry camping and hiking. Open daily from 8:00 a.m.–noon, and from 1:00–5:00 p.m. Call (520) 638-7875 (Monday–Friday, 1–5 p.m.) for more information.

Desert View Information Station (Desert View): Open year-round. At the end of Desert View Drive (formerly East Rim Drive), you'll find Desert View, where there's a bookstore operated by the Grand Canyon Association and an NPS information station. Here you can get books, maps, and Park Service publications. Call (520) 638-7893 for more information.

NORTH RIM AND INNER CANYON

North Rim Visitor Center (Bright Angel Point parking area): Open May 15–October 15. Located at the south end of the Bright Angel Point parking area, this facility provides orientation materials, maps, brochures, backcountry trip planning information, and a bookstore. You can also join ranger-led activities. Call (520) 638-7864 for more information.

Backcountry Information Center (North Rim Ranger Station): Open May 15–October 31. Located just north of the main North Rim campground, this office issues backcountry permits and provides visitors with information on camping and hiking. Open daily from 8:00 a.m.–noon. Call (520) 638-7875 for more information.

Transportation Desk (at the Grand Canyon Lodge): Open May 15–October 15. This desk in the lobby of the Grand Canyon Lodge provides information on daily commercial tours available during the season. Call (520) 638-2612 for more information.

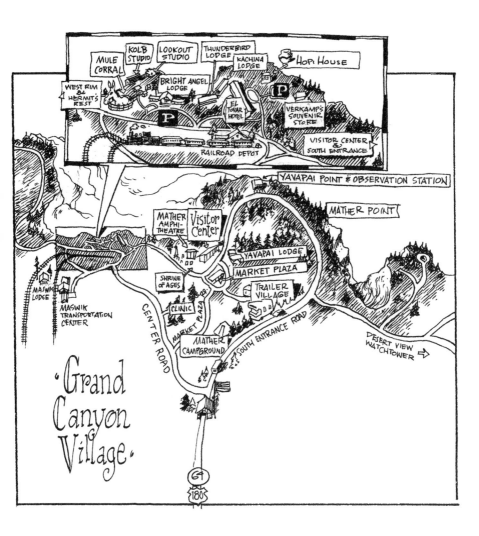

MULE CORRAL

KOLB STUDIO

LOOKOUT STUDIO

THUNDERBIRD LODGE

KACHINA LODGE

HOPI HOUSE

WEST RIM & HERMIT'S REST

BRIGHT ANGEL LODGE

P

EL TOVAR HOTEL

P

VERKAMP'S SOUVENIR STORE

RAILROAD DEPOT

VISITOR CENTER & SOUTH ENTRANCE

YAVAPAI POINT & OBSERVATION STATION

MATHER AMPHI-THEATRE

Visitor Center

MATHER POINT

YAVAPAI LODGE

MARKET PLAZA

MASWIK LODGE

SHRINE OF AGES

TRAILER VILLAGE

MASWIK TRANSPORTATION CENTER

CLINIC

MARKET PLAZA RD.

SOUTH ENTRANCE ROAD

DESERT VIEW WATCHTOWER →

CENTER ROAD

MATHER CAMPGROUND

'Grand Canyon Village'

64 180

What is the Colorado Plateau?

TOU
ARE
HERE
↓

It's hard to imagine that the Grand Canyon and its plateaus are just a small part of a much larger geologic region called the Colorado Plateau, which encompasses diverse landscapes like deep canyons, towering volcanic mountains, and seven massive plateaus. Elevations in the region range from 5,000 feet to about 12,700 feet above sea level. The Colorado Plateau is bounded by the Mogollon Rim on the south, the Painted Desert and Echo Cliffs on the east, the high plateaus of southern Utah on the north, and the Grand Wash Cliffs on the west. The region comprises five national parks, four national monuments, parts of two national recreation areas, two national forests, two Bureau of Land Management districts, five sovereign Indian nations, numerous wilderness areas, and parts of four states.

The Colorado Plateau is considered a geologic province, a region whose rock formations and landforms share a common history that sets it apart from neighboring regions. Here you'll find one of the most varied assortments of isolated buttes, mesas, odd landforms, and remarkable scenery in the world. Most of the region sits atop thousands of sedimentary rock layers born from ancient seas that advanced and retreated over millions of years. Over long periods of time, these deposits were reshaped through the uplift, tilting, and folding of the earth's crust. Today, the rocks are exposed by the deep canyons that dissect the region and by the sparseness of soil cover and vegetation. That's why the Colorado Plateau provides geologists with an unequaled record of much of the earth's history.

It's also an area where animals, plants, minerals, water, and climate work together in dynamic synchronicity. From a "big picture" point of view, the Colorado Plateau is a very large, interconnected whole that doesn't separate Grand Canyon National Park from the lands that surround it. And, once you take away all the man-made boundaries and put everything together, you have nearly 100 million acres of interactive system that includes a unique landscape, wild animals, and plants that depend upon one another to stay alive—not to mention the million or so human residents who love it. The Colorado Plateau is home to a fascinating mix of cultures, some dating back thousands of years, which are still evident today in the region's Indian nations.

The animals that call this ecosystem home—the desert bighorn sheep, pronghorned antelope, prairie dogs, and others—have adapted over a long period of time to the harsh living conditions and rugged terrain by changing their behavior according to time of day and weather. Animals aren't the only travelers within the region. Plants migrate as well, although they "travel" more slowly as they're carried by animals or weather. The flora and fauna evolved together, surviving cooperatively despite the harshness of the environment.

For the visitor, the Colorado Plateau means more than 130,000 square miles of spectacular scenic and wildland opportunities. It's a place where you can pitch a tent, fish or boat in one of many rivers and lakes, view some of the country's most beautiful landscapes and wildlife, and enjoy many outdoor activities. Besides the Grand Canyon, the area also offers visitors Zion and Bryce Canyons, Cedar Breaks, Glen Canyon, Rainbow Bridge, the Canyonlands, Capitol Reef, Arches, Four Corners, Mesa Verde, Petrified Forest, the Painted Desert, San Francisco Peaks, and Oak Creek Canyon, among many other natural wonders. As I guide you through this beautiful park, I'll also give you tips on exploring beyond the park, inside the boundaries of the Colorado Plateau.

For more information on the Colorado Plateau area, contact the Grand Canyon Trust, 2601 N. Fort Valley Road, Flagstaff, AZ, 86001. Or, call (520) 774-7488 (phone) or (520) 774-7570 (fax).

To get you started, here's what's included in the Colorado Plateau area:

NATIONAL PARKS, MONUMENTS, FORESTS, RECREATION AREAS
Grand Canyon National Park
Zion National Park
Bryce National Park
Canyonlands National Park
Arches National Park
Sunset Crater National Monument
Wupatki National Monument
Pipe Spring National Monument
Walnut Canyon National Monument
Lake Mead National Recreation Area
Glen Canyon National Recreation Area
Coconino National Forest
Kaibab National Forest

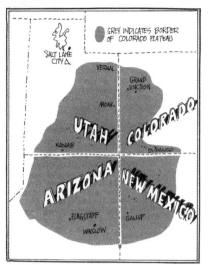

GREY INDICATES BORDER OF COLORADO PLATEAU

SALT LAKE CITY
VERNAL
GRAND JUNCTION
MOAB
UTAH
COLORADO
KANAB
DURANGO
ARIZONA
NEW MEXICO
FLAGSTAFF
GALLUP
WINSLOW

TRIBAL LANDS
Hualapai Reservation
Havasupai Reservation
Navajo Reservation
Hopi Reservation
Kaibab Paiute Reservation

PRIVATELY-OWNED LANDS

STATE-OWNED LANDS

GRAND CANYON FACTS

- Area: 1.2 million acres or 1,904 square miles
- Length: 277 river miles (Lees Ferry to Grand Wash Cliffs)
- Minimum aerial width: 600 feet at Navajo Bridge (near Lees Ferry)
- Average Rim to Rim aerial width: 10 miles
- Maximum Rim to Rim aerial width: 18 miles
- Average depth: 1 mile
- Total miles of trails in park: 500
- Miles of maintained trails: 33
- Average temperatures (degrees Fahrenheit):
  South Rim:
  Low: 18° (January)
  High: 85° (July)
  North Rim:
  Low: 15° (January)
  High: 77° (July)
  Inner Canyon:
  Low: 38° (January)
  High: 105° (July)
- Growth in annual visitation:

Year	Number of visitors
1919	44,173
1930	166,711
1940	369,234
1950	665,281
1956	1,033,404
	(first year to exceed 1 million visitors)
1970	2,258,195
1980	2,618,713
1990	3,752,901
1997	4,851,931

- Rim elevations (in feet):
  South Rim:
  El Tovar 6,920
  Mather Point 7,120
  Grandview Point 7,400
  Desert View 7,500
  Bright Angel Trailhead . . 6,850
  South Kaibab Trailhead . . 7,200
  North Rim:
  Grand Canyon Lodge . . . 8,200
  Point Imperial 8,800
  Cape Royal 7,865
  North Kaibab Trailhead . . 8,240
  Inner Canyon:
  Indian Garden 3,800
  Phantom Ranch 2,400
  Roaring Springs 5,000

Side Canons of the Colorado, engraving, Ives Expedition
Photo courtesy Grand Canyon National Park
Museum Collection, #16240

28

How was the Grand Canyon formed?

You won't find much agreement on exactly how the canyon was formed. However, geologists who have spent time studying the area seem to agree on many points. Here's the short version of a very long story.

Geologists agree that about 2 billion years ago, during the Precambrian era, the future Grand Canyon was at the bottom of an ancient and mostly lifeless sea. For tens of millions of years there had been successive layering of sand, silt, and clay deposits from adjacent continental lands. Volcanic action contributed lava and ash to these deposits. The deposits accumulated over time, and later found themselves buried deep in the earth, where the intense pressure and heat converted the sedimentary rocks to metamorphic rock. The Vishnu schist is an example of this; originally it was a mostly horizontal layered group of sand, shales, mudstones, and volcanics. Metamorphism created a nearly molten mass of twisted and folded material that bore little resemblance to its original state. The cause of all this was a collision about 1.7 billion years ago of two or more continental masses bordering the Grand Canyon region, which probably resulted in construction of a major mountain chain similar to the present-day Rocky Mountains.

As the mountains grew upward and plate collisions waxed and waned, the forces of erosion began their relentless work on the layers of sedimentary deposits in the area that was to become the Grand Canyon. Evidence of this is now shown by the late Precambrian rocks of the Grand Canyon Supergroup. These horizontal rocks were uplifted, tilted, and eroded. Then younger sediments were deposited over these tilted rocks, which were by now deeply buried and changed by heat and pressure to solid rock. Again, uplift brought these rocks to the surface, where the process of erosion could continue its work. Begun in the Paleozoic era, this process of uplift and erosion continued up to some 250 million years ago.

Around 65 million years ago there was a regional uplift that marked the beginnings of the Rocky Mountains, as well as the Colorado Plateau. This general uplift, which probably continues to the present, resulted in the removal of many thousands of feet of sediments covering the present-day Grand Canyon.

Some six million years ago, volcanic activity broke out in the region, leaving lava flows, spectacular volcanic peaks, and cinder cones that we find throughout the area today. This activity appears to have ended in 1064 A.D.

About one million years ago there was a massive lava flow in the western Grand Canyon that dammed the canyon for several hundred years, and a caused water to back up to around Moab, Utah. The base of this lava flow was only a few dozen feet above the present-day river bed of the Colorado, indicating that the canyon was close to its present depth. During this same time period, the Grand Canyon was eventually carved by a rising land mass now called the Kaibab uplift.

It's at this point in geologic time that geologists disagree on how the Grand Canyon was actually formed. Although most geologists agree that the canyon was carved by at least two major streams, which eventually joined to form the Colorado River, the stage was now set for the numerous modern theories on the final carving of the Grand Canyon.

One of the most plausible theories has stream systems beginning to flow into the newly formed Gulf of California and quickly eroding westward into the Colorado Plateau, eventually capturing the ancestral Colorado River somewhere west of the Kaibab uplift. This theory suggests that different sections of the Grand Canyon have different ages, formed by two or more river systems.

So there is a long, deep central canyon occupied by the Colorado River. What about the width of the Grand Canyon? Local erosion carved out the side canyons, in all their glory, and the Colorado River acted like a giant conveyor belt to carry the material to the Gulf of California. Through a long process of simple erosion by rainfall, freeze and thaw, gravity, and many other tools, a deep canyon was turned into a Grand Canyon.

What we know is that the forces that created the Grand Canyon worked, sometimes slowly and sometimes in the blink of an eye, over millions of years. Even today, they are at work in the form of rockfalls, landslides, and flash floods that continue to widen the canyon, while the Colorado River strives to lower its bed to sea level. Someday, in the future, these agents of erosion combined with the slowing of downcutting by the Colorado as it nears sea level, could create a broad valley with a slow-moving stream where once there was a grand canyon.

If you're interested in reading the whole story of how the Grand Canyon was formed, get a copy of *A Field Guide to the Grand Canyon* by Stephen R. Whitney, or a copy of *An Introduction to Grand Canyon Geology* by L. Greer Price.

STEPS IN THE CREATION OF THE GRAND CANYON

1 Pressure within the earth slowly uplifted the surface, causing rivers to run deeper and faster. As the channels deepened, land on both sides was eroded into the river, and the canyon took a V-shape.

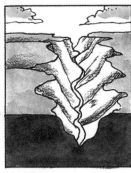

2 Erosion worked with many tools, including rain, freeze, and thaw to break down the sides of the main and tributary canyons even further, creating an ever-widening canyon.

3 Over millions of years, the deepening of the river slowed, while the widening continued. In time, the canyon wall may disappear, leaving a flat plain.

Why is there only **one** Grand Canyon?

If you've ever traveled across the United States or the world, you've probably seen other canyons like the Grand Canyon—just not as big, or with so many wildly different landforms, or with such a range of colors. The name Grand Canyon is fitting in that it's the only one to combine all these elements on such a, well, grand scale. To understand why, you have to look at five main factors that have combined to make this canyon unique in the world.

Geography: You start with a desert climate that has a very powerful river system—in this case, the Colorado and its ancestors—running through it.

Geology: You then add a mile or so of horizontal or nearly horizontal sedimentary rock layers. It is believed that, at one time, thousands of feet of sedimentary rock covered the Grand Canyon region.

Major Geologic Event: Then figure in a major regional uplift allowing the rivers to cut downward through the horizontal rocks. This uplift created the Colorado Plateau, which covers much of the Four Corners region.

Time: You also add just enough time to allow the river system to do its work of eroding the sedimentary rocks, but not so much time that the area has been reduced to sea-level lowlands.

Exposure: Nowhere else in the world is such an authentic geologic record of time visible on such a grand scale as at the Grand Canyon. As you look at the many layers of rocks and the many colors splashed against the Canyon walls, and consider the centuries upon centuries it took to form, you begin to understand the enormous feat called the Grand Canyon.

Here's a chart describing the different layers:

	ESTIMATED AGE MILLIONS OF YEARS
RIM	
KAIBAB LIMESTONE	250
TOROWEAP	260
COCONINO SANDSTONE	270
HERMIT SHALE	280
SUPAI GROUP	300
SURPRISE CANYON FORMATION	320
REDWALL LIMESTONE	330
TEMPLE BUTTE	370
UNDIVIDED DOLOMITE	500
MUAV LIMESTONE	530
BRIGHT ANGEL SHALE	540
TAPEATS SANDSTONE	550
GRAND CANYON SUPER GROUP	800 MILLION TO 1.2 BILLION YEARS
VISHNU SCHIST	

33

What's so special about canyon nights?

Far away from the glare of big city lights and pollution, the recurring drama of the night sky over the Grand Canyon is hard to describe. During the full moon, the Canyon comes alive with looming shadows that transform the Inner Canyon. The new moon lifts the veil of the Milky Way and reveals the glow of infinite stars emblazoned across a black universe. On moonless nights, the Canyon is dark beyond compare. With no streetlights, you're lucky to see your hand in front of your face, much less a trail or a sidewalk. Remember, a flashlight will be your best friend on these nights.

Here are some suggestions for experiencing Canyon nights:

South Rim. This is where you'll find the most popular and crowded spots for experiencing Canyon nights. Because it's so dark, the safest spots include the open areas around the hotels along the rim (although exterior lighting may spoil the impact). More adventuresome night watchers can try Mather, Yavapai, Pima, and Hopi Points. Walking the trail from El Tovar to Yavapai Point at night is an entirely different experience than it is during the day. Dress warm, stay on the trail, carry a flashlight—and don't forget to stop and look up every so often.

North Rim. Because of its orientation, dense tree cover, and fewer established trails, the North Rim offers fewer opportunities for viewing Canyon nights than the South Rim. The exceptions are the open areas around the Grand Canyon Lodge; the veranda at the Lodge offers great views. One of the North Rim's finest experiences is the walk to Bright Angel Point on a moonlit night. The shadowed Canyon becomes otherworldly, and you can see the far-off twinkling lights of the South Rim Village.

Where are the best spots to see a sunrise and sunset over the Canyon?

Definitely along the rim. Although most visitors would say there's no one "best" spot to see the sun rise and fall over the Canyon, I can tell you some of the most popular spots, as well as some of my favorites.

South Rim. This is where you'll find the most popular, and crowded, spots for viewing a spectacular sunrise over the Canyon. Some of the most popular spots include open areas around the hotels along the rim, and Yaki, Yavapai, Mather, and Hopi Points. The most crowded of the overlooks on any given summer day is Mather Point. For outstanding sunset views, you can try around the hotels, or Yavapai, Hopi, and Pima Points. My choice for experiencing an unparalleled sunrise is Mather Point, and Lipan Point for a spectacular sunset. You can find your own "favorite spot" by picking almost any point along the South Rim that has sweeping views to the east and west.

North Rim. Because of its orientation, the North Rim's fewer established trails offer more limited opportunities for viewing sunrise and sunset. The exceptions are the open areas around the Grand Canyon Lodge (even the veranda at the Lodge offers great views), Bright Angel Point, the Cape Royal picnic area, and Point Imperial, where you'll be treated to a great sunrise.

Here's a summary of times for sunrise and sunset at the Grand Canyon. Don't forget to arrive early at your viewing spot. Now, let's go sun hunting!

	S U N R I S E	S U N S E T
JANUARY	7:31 a.m.–7:40 a.m.	5:24 p.m.–5:53 p.m.
FEBRUARY	7:01 a.m.–7:30 a.m.	5:54 p.m.–6:21 p.m.
MARCH	6:17 a.m.– 6:59 a.m.	6:22 p.m.– 6:48 p.m.
APRIL	5:37 a.m.–6:15 a.m.	6:49 p.m.–7:14 p.m.
MAY	5:13 a.m.–5:36 a.m.	7:15 p.m.–7:39 p.m.
JUNE	5:10 a.m.–5:14 a.m.	7:39 p.m.–7:49 p.m.
JULY	5:14 a.m.–5:32 a.m.	7:34 p.m.–7:49 p.m.
AUGUST	5:34 a.m.–5:58 a.m.	6:58 p.m.–7:33 p.m.
SEPTEMBER	5:59 a.m.–6:21 a.m.	6:14 p.m.–6:57 p.m.
OCTOBER	6:22 a.m.–6:49 a.m.	5:34 p.m.–6:13 p.m.
NOVEMBER	6:50 a.m.–7:19 a.m.	5:14 p.m.–5:32 p.m.
DECEMBER	7:20 a.m.–7:39 a.m.	5:13 p.m.–5:23 p.m.

Where can we see Waterfalls?

Although there are numerous waterfalls in Grand Canyon National Park, most require so much effort and time to get to that you'll need from three to seven days to see them. The exception is the Roaring Springs waterfall and picnic area, which can be accessed by hiking 4.7 miles down the North Kaibab Trail from the North Rim. For more information about this trail, call the North Rim Visitor Center (open May 15–October 15) at (520) 638-7864.

The waterfalls that are the easiest to reach from the South Rim are located in the Canyon, but outside park boundaries. This spectacular series of four, blue-green waterfalls can be found on the Havasupai Indian Reservation in the western Grand Canyon, near the village of Supai. This is one of the most beautiful and remote areas of the Canyon, and is accessible only by foot, on horseback, or by limited helicopter service.

The trail to the village of Supai begins at Hualapai Hilltop, which is 66 miles from Peach Springs, Arizona. Peach Springs is on old Highway 66, north of Interstate 40. Driving time from Grand Canyon Village on the South Rim to Hualapai Hilltop is approximately four to five hours. Special permits to visit the reservation and village of Supai are required, and cost $12 per person November–March, and $15 per person April–October. You can obtain a permit by calling the Havasupai Tourist Enterprise at (520) 448-2121, or (520) 448-2141.

Getting to the village of Supai by foot means an eight-mile walk down a large tributary canyon on the south side of the Colorado River. While the hike down to the village is easy to moderate, be sure you take plenty of water and rest often, especially during the hot weather. The trip by saddle and pack horses is less strenuous—except for the horses and mules—and takes three to four hours. Cost is approximately $50 one-way, $80 round-trip from the Hilltop to Supai Village, or $110 to the campground. If you're planning to travel on foot or by saddle and pack horses, allow at least three days for the trip. That way, you'll be able to spend one entire day exploring and enjoying the falls.

Helicopter service to the village of Supai is available most Fridays and Sundays. For more information, call Airwest Helicopters of Arizona at (520) 516-2790. For special charters from the Grand Canyon Airport to Supai Village, call Papillon Grand Canyon Helicopters at (800) 528-2418.

In the village of Supai is the Havasupai Lodge, with year-round overnight accommodations. A cafe in the village serves breakfast, lunch, and dinner. From the village, the falls are a short, easy walk down Havasu Canyon. Distances from the village to the falls are: Navajo Falls, 1.5 miles; Havasu Falls and campground, 2 miles; Mooney Falls, 3 miles; and Beaver Falls, 5 miles. From Beaver Falls the trail continues another 4 miles until it reaches the Colorado River. There are many places along the trail to picnic, so plan for an entire day to enjoy one of the most beautiful walks you'll ever take. Here are the numbers to call for more information on rates and reservations: Tourist Office and Havasupai Campground, (520) 448-2121; and Havasupai Lodge, (520) 448-2111.

Havasu Falls.

Since the Grand Canyon ranges from 1,200 feet at the Canyon's western floor to 9,200 feet on the North Rim, it is home to a unique variety of animals that are indigenous to both desert and mountain environments. These extreme elevation changes in a relatively small area support a wide range of habitats, from aquatic to desert scrub to coniferous forest, that would normally be found only by traveling from Mexico to Canada. Now, let's take a look at the inhabitants.

Of the 300 species of birds that have been observed at the Grand Canyon, 136 nest in the area and 40 live there year-round, including the double-crested cormorant, great blue heron, mallard duck, red-tailed hawk, Peregrine falcon, Gambel's quail, mourning dove, great horned owl, and canyon wren.

There are 4 species of native fish that still live in the Grand Canyon stretch of the Colorado River. Their numbers have decreased due to damming, but there is a small remnant population at the junction of the Colorado and Little Colorado Rivers. They include the humpback chub, flannelmouth sucker, bluehead sucker, and speckled dace. The park also has 7 types of frogs, toads, and salamanders who are year-round residents, including the Utah tiger salamander, Rocky Mountain toad, and canyon tree frog. Hikers will rarely see any of our 41 kinds of reptiles, including the northern plateau lizard, mountain short-horned lizard, Sonoran gopher snake, California kingsnake, and the very-seldom-seen pinkish Grand Canyon rattlesnake, which is found only in the Inner Canyon.

Of our 70 different types of mammals, 11 species are found only on the North Rim, and 9 only on the South Rim. The most famous of these are 2 species of tassel-eared squirrels, which are quite similar except for coloration on their undersides and tails. The Kaibab squirrel of the North Rim is found nowhere else in the world. The Abert squirrel of the South Rim has been seen as far north as Colorado and as far south as Mexico. It seems as though the little Abert squirrel must have crossed over to the North Rim at one point when pine trees were more plentiful. Later, as the climate became more arid and the pines retreated to higher elevations, the squirrels on the North Rim were isolated from their kin and slowly evolved into a different species.

Of the more abundant mammals, here are some that you might expect to see when you visit the Grand Canyon. On the rims, look for the rock pocket mouse, the nocturnal ringtail cat (which looks like a wide-eyed raccoon), western spotted skunk (look for them between the Bright Angel Lodge and El Tovar Hotel during the summer), wild turkey, mule deer, elk, and coyote. In the Inner Canyon, you might see the desert bighorn on the Bright Angel and Kaibab Trails just below the South Rim, California bat, white-tailed antelope, canyon mouse, and desert wood rat. With the exception of squirrels, many of the smaller animals are hard to find because they escape the daytime heat in burrows, caves, rock crevices, tree cavities, and other shady areas. Many of them are partly nocturnal, coming out during the cool night for food. As a result, the predatory animals are also nocturnal. Canyon animals have adapted very well to the harsh environment by beating the heat.

Water is the primary necessity for the survival of Grand Canyon animals, and they have developed clever ways of getting it. Smaller animals that don't have the ability to search widely for water, including squirrels, mice, and kangaroo rats, are able to get enough water from the food they eat or as part of the normal process of digesting their food. An interesting example of adaptation to the desert environment is the antelope ground squirrel, which supplements its primarily vegetarian diet with insects, thereby increasing its moisture supply. You might say that the Grand Canyon has bred a bunch of smart, year-round inhabitants.

What are the best ways to spot wildlife?

Looking for animals in the hot, arid climate of the Grand Canyon can be a challenging task, since many animals use hiding places to escape the heat. It requires time, patience, and cunning observation.

The first thing to know about our desert residents is that they feed in the early morning and early evening hours. To better your chances of seeing wildlife, try walking the rim in the morning when there's still a chill in the air, or take a walk just before or after sunset. These are also the best times to lose the crowds, which tend to frighten away our quiet desert animals. Wear fabrics that blend naturally with the desert colors. If you're walking, move slowly, and if you see an animal, avoid sudden movements. Don't forget binoculars for an up-close view. Most importantly, don't try to get too close to the animals.

Here are some hints about places to view certain animals. Year-round, look for the tassel-eared Abert squirrel feeding on the tender shoots and pine cones of the tall ponderosa pines throughout the South Rim. The Kaibab squirrel, a close relative of the Abert, thrives in the ponderosa pine forests of the North Rim. In the developed areas along the rims you'll probably run into rock squirrels begging for food handouts from visitors. If you're hiking, keep an eye out for our more elusive predator, the bobcat, who frequents the North and South Rims. A more common sight is the coyote, hunting throughout the park from rim to river. The most commonly seen mammal on the South Rim is the mule deer, who travels in and out of the Canyon with great speed and agility.

One of the largest hoofed mammals in the park, the desert bighorn, prefers the rocky slopes of the Inner Canyon to the rim. Like other mammals of the desert, they are most likely to be seen near sources of water like springs, seeps, or pools of summer rain.

The handsome, non-poisonous gopher snake is the only snake you're likely to see along the rim. If you're walking in open rocky areas

Wake up, honey. Time to go see the deer feeding.

NNNNH!

near the rim you might also catch a glimpse of the southern plateau lizard, with a blue patch on either side of its throat.

The birds you'll see most frequently are the mountain chickadee, with its black bib and white stripe over its eye, and the nuthatch, deftly flying through the coniferous forests along the rims in search of insects. Look to the sky if you're standing on the rim during the summer months, and you might glimpse a white-throated swift or violet-green swallow slashing through the air in pursuit of insects. Or, you might hear the distinctive caw of the black raven flying in the canyon or perched along the rim.

But remember, when you feed wild animals, you're not doing them a favor. In fact, many of the animals that have become habituated to human food at the Grand Canyon end up starving to death because they have ingested foods that they can't process. Please help keep our animals wild and healthy by not feeding them.

BIGHORNS AND BURROS IN THE GRAND CANYON

Between the late 1860s and early 1900s, miners and prospectors arrived in the Grand Canyon in search of the copper, silver, lead, zinc, uranium, and asbestos that had been discovered in the area. To get heavy equipment and supplies in and out of the Canyon, miners used sturdy burros as pack animals. As mining activity in the area ended, mining claims were abandoned and burros were left behind, and eventually became a feral population of thousands.

The burros' progeny created an ecological nightmare in the latter part of the 1900s, when an ever-increasing burro population began competing for the same resources used by the bighorn sheep and other indigenous animals. Burro Canyon in the park is so named because of the thousands of burros that used to flock to the site for water.

As the wild burros flourished, the population of bighorn sheep decreased dramatically. In the late 1970s to early 1980s, most of the burros were captured and removed from the Grand Canyon through the efforts of the National Park Service and private humane societies. Removal activities peaked in 1980–1981, with a major effort by the Fund for Animals to round up all remaining burros.

Today, bighorn sheep in the park have again become a stable and healthy population, and burros can still be found in several remote canyons of the Hualapai and Havasupai Indian Reservations.

Sorry, no petting zoo privileges here. Every time someone feeds an animal at the Grand Canyon, a little bit of the "wild" is stolen from our wildlife. Human food can not only damage the animals' health, but also endanger their survival by luring them away from their natural habitats.

Feeding one of our cute chipmunks or squirrels and capturing the moment on film might seem like a good idea, but their teeth are sharp and there's always the possibility of infection. In the case of a wild animal bite, doctors usually recommend a series of painful rabies shots. Not a fun way to spend your vacation.

Federal law prohibits people from feeding or approaching our wildlife, and for good reason. Our animals may look harmless, but most are capable of causing injury, and in extreme cases even death, to people who get too close. If an animal reacts to your presence, you're probably too close.

Besides, you can learn more about animal habits through quiet observation than interaction. For good photographs of animals, take a look at the huge selection of books and postcards in the stores throughout the park.

What are the most dangerous animals?

Yep, you guessed it: chipmunks and squirrels. Okay, maybe it wasn't your first guess. Nevertheless, the same cute little critters you try to feed and photograph on the rock walls between Verkamp's and the Bright Angel Lodge have the distinction of being the Grand Canyon's most notorious biters. They're especially ornery when people try to lure them by pretending to have food, just to get a good picture. Year-round, the most dangerous animal in the Grand Canyon is the one you try to feed.

You also can run into these little critters on the trail. If you set your pack down on a heavily traveled trail such as Bright Angel, it's an open invitation to ground squirrels. They can rip a hole in an expensive pack in the time it takes to take a sip of water.

In the canyon, scorpions are common, and stings often occur. The good news is: while scorpion stings are painful, they rarely cause serious health problems. If stung, apply cold compresses for pain relief and monitor any symptoms. The bad news is: scorpions are small and hard to see, due to their light tan color. If you're camping or backpacking, shake out boots, clothing, and bedding before getting into them.

Although the reclusive bobcat and rarely seen mountain lion naturally avoid contact with humans, they are wild animals and caution should always be used when you're in their habitat. Keep an eye on your kids, who may think it's fun to run out of your sight, and unknowingly into the path of a wild animal. Even mule deer can be dangerous if surprised. The other animals to watch out for are the coyote, who appears to be unafraid of people; the raven, who is not shy about taking food right out of people's backpacks; and the occasional black bear on the North Rim.

Most injuries at the Canyon result from people getting too close to animals. The moral is, don't be fooled into thinking the cute little ones are harmless. Fleas carried by ground squirrels have been known to spread disease. And remember, any animal that begs for food is potentially dangerous. Let's just say it's best if people and animals at the Canyon maintain a long-distance relationship.

43

The most important thing to know is that even though they're around, you probably won't see many snakes and lizards at the Grand Canyon. Also, they are rarely found above 7,000 feet. Although they are well suited for life in the desert, most reptiles escape the heat by burrowing underground or hiding in shaded rock crevices, coming out to forage during the cooler morning and early evening hours. Several Canyon species are nocturnal. Most of the snakes in the Canyon, with the exception of several species of rattlesnake, are harmless to humans.

Most Grand Canyon reptiles hibernate to avoid the winter cold. That's why you'll almost never see snakes on the higher plateaus, where temperatures are coldest. Reptiles are most abundant in the lower, warmer zones of the Inner Canyon. If you're walking in the Canyon in the early morning, you might see snakes and lizards warming themselves on rocks or on open ground exposed to the sun. A chuckwalla will bask in the sun on ledges, and, if threatened, will slip into a crack in the rock and puff up, making it extremely difficult to dislodge him. At dusk, you might spot reptiles in places that have retained the day's heat, like stones or pavement.

REPTILES

Reptiles at the Canyon come in a wide variety of lizards and snakes. There are even three subspecies of rattlesnake that are found only at the Grand Canyon. These include the rarely seen Grand Canyon rattlesnake, with its pinkish color and diamond-shaped pattern on its skin. It's found in the Inner Canyon and has a distinctive rattle. The Hopi rattlesnake, which lives in the Inner Canyon and along the South Rim, is pinkish, greenish, or grayish in color, with well-defined splotches. The Great Basin rattlesnake is found in the Inner Canyon or along the North Rim. Color varies from light brown to gray, with dark, well-defined, narrow splotches.

Although you may never see one, reptiles—both harmless and venomous—are a natural part of the landscape of the Grand Canyon.

Chuckwalla

Any great birding spots?

Although the Grand Canyon is more famous for rocks than birds, it still has more than its share of feathered residents. Throughout the year, 315 species of birds call the Canyon home (with 136 known species that nest here), including 21 kinds of hawks, eagles, and falcons. The birds range in size from the tiny Rufous hummingbird and Bell's Vireo to the great blue heron and California condor.

For avid birders, there is a vast array of interesting birds and habitats to choose from in and around the Grand Canyon, including 66 species that live here year-round. While some of our desert species depend upon open water for moisture, many birds get enough from the insects they eat.The best way to see the greatest number of birds at the Grand Canyon is to visit a variety of habitats; and that means hiking. A day hike to Indian Garden or an overnight hike to Phantom Ranch offers a wonderful variety of birds. Here are some other areas you might want to check out.

Let's start with aquatic habitats with standing water along the rims. This includes the sewage lagoons (artificial ponds that have become popular resting spots for migrating birds and provide some great birding opportunities) and cattle tanks on the South Rim, and lakes on the North Rim (from May to November). In the summer, you'll probably see the violet-green swallow and the spotted sandpiper at the ponds and tanks as well as all over both rims. If you're lucky, you might also catch a glimpse of a migrating double-crested cormorant, great blue heron, or mallard duck around the ponds.

Along both rims in the pinyon pine and ponderosa pine forests mixed with firs, aspens, spruce, and oaks above 7000 feet, some of the most common-ly seen birds include the red-tailed hawk, American kestrel, mourning dove (summers), great horned owl, common raven, the rock and canyon wren, the western bluebird, and the American robin. Other commonly seen birds along the rims include the mountain chickadee, white brested nuthatch, dark-eyed junco, juniper tit-mouse, as well as the Steller's and west-ern scrub jay. If you're here in the summer, you might catch a glimpse of the house finch, brown-headed cowbird, black-chinned hum-mingbird, and the turkey vulture.

Throughout September and October, keep a special watch out for the numerous species of raptors that migrate through the area. During the winter months, look for the white-crowned sparrow. All along the South Rim is prime bird watching territory, especially along the abyss on the West Rim where you might see peregrine falcons flying high overhead. On the North Rim you can also expect to see wild turkey, Clark's nutcracker, and perhaps a Williamson's sapsucker.

As you go down the Canyon you're likely to see many of the same species in habitats ranging from the grasslands of the Toroweap Valley and meadows of the Kaibab Plateau (4600 feet) to Mohave and Sonoran desert scrub (below 2000 feet).

At the lower elevations of the canyon you'll find aquatic habitats with flowing water including the Colorado River and its tributaries such as Bright Angel and Garden Creeks. In the summer, look for the blue-winged teal and spotted sandpiper, common sights on the river. During the winter months, look for the bald eagle along the banks of the river and its tributaries. Riparian woodland habitats along the banks of the Colorado River and its tributaries are home to feathered residents like the Lucy's warbler, Bell's vireo, willow flycatcher, hood-ed oriole, and blue grosbeak.

That should get you started. Don't forget to take along a pair of binoculars for viewing our feathered residents. If you want to read more about birds in the Grand Canyon, I recommend *A Field Guide to the Grand Canyon* by Stephen R. Whitney.

CONDORS IN THE CANYON

If you are lucky during your visit to the Grand Canyon, you might catch a glimpse of a rare and majestic bird, the California condor. These gigantic birds, with nearly ten-foot wingspans, were more common in this area in the past; but shootings, poisonings, and collisions with power lines drastically reduced their numbers.

In 1996, six condors were released in the Vermilion Cliffs just west of Lees Ferry. Since then, more condors have been released in other nearby areas. A small number of these birds currently inhabit the Canyon environment. All of them have been reintroduced from other locations, thanks to the combined efforts of the Peregrine Fund, the U.S. Fish and Wildlife Service, the Arizona Game and Fish Department, the National Park Service, and the U.S. Bureau of Land Management.

All of the condors in the Grand Canyon area carry wing tags to allow research staff to track and identify particular birds. Another identifying factor is that condors have no feathers on their heads. Young condors have a black head color, while adult condors have an orange head color.

Young condors are curious birds and may be attracted to human environments such as campsites, so avoid damage to your belongings by not leaving equipment unattended. If you are lucky enough to encounter a condor, do not approach or attempt to feed the bird. Please report anyone seen harassing or harming a condor to park management.

For additional information about the California condor relocation project, please call the Peregrine Fund at (520) 355-2270, the Arizona Game & Fish Department at (520) 774-5045, or try online at www.peregrinefund.org for an excellent source of up-to-date information (they even give bios for each bird).

Just as the Canyon supports a diversity of animal life, so too does it host an array of plants. At every elevation you will see plant life adapted to the various life zones represented in the Canyon. Let's take a look at the major categories of plants that are found in the Grand Canyon, and find out where they grow.

FERNS AND RELATED PLANTS

The ferns and allied plants like horsetails and spike moss are among the oldest in the fossil record. Of the earth's 10,000 types of ferns and related plants, about 20 are found in the Grand Canyon. Because of the steep terrain, many Canyon ferns are adapted to growing in cliff crevices, where enough soil and moisture are found. A few grow in moist places like seeps, springs, and stream banks, while others prefer more arid habitats like the Canyon's limestone cliffs. Near streams, ponds, springs, and especially the Colorado River, you'll see horsetails and scouring rushes.

Male Fern

Look for the maidenhair fern near seeps and springs below the rims, and brittle fern in the nearby rocky areas. In moist crevices throughout the Canyon walls, look for Eaton's lip ferns. In the more arid habitats, like the dry rocky slopes and cliffs below the rim, you'll find the slender lip and the lip fern, the most abundant dry-habitat fern in the park. In the limestone rocks below the rim, keep an eye out for the wavy cloak fern. In the North Rim forests, you'll find western bracken.

FLOWERING PLANTS

With its varied topography and climate, the Grand Canyon supports over 1,500 species of flowering

Golden Columbine

plants, including annuals, perennials, wildflowers, cacti, and trees and shrubs. These are normal plants that have adapted themselves to the dry, blistering temperatures of the Inner Gorge and the snowy, freezing winters of the Kaibab Plateau. In a word, they're "tough"! Plants that live in the scorching areas of the Inner Canyon grow far apart from each other to minimize competition for water. Most desert wildflowers adapt to the climate by blooming only in the early spring, when soils are moist and temperatures mild. If rainfall is below normal, they may even remain dormant for several years. Most of the plants that grow in the Inner Canyon have adapted to heat and drought by modifying their leaves and stems. That's why you'll see many Canyon plants that have small, coated leaves, hair and thorns, special root systems, and succulents that store moisture in leaves and stems.

On the high plateaus where temperatures dip below freezing even on summer nights, the plants become dormant during the winter (with the first snows of autumn) and put out rapid shoots at the first hint of summer (shortly after the snowpack melts).

Desert Tobacco

Here are some of the flowering plants that are commonly seen along the South and North Rims: the prickle poppy, sego lily, rock mat, bristly hiddenflower, Wheeler's thistle, Rocky Mountain pussytoe, sulfur flower, bladderpod, stickleaf, broom snakeweed, skyrocket, carmine thistle, perennial rock cress, wire lettuce, hill lupine, toadflax penstemon, green gentian, deers ears, specklepod, and tidy fleabane. Below the rims look for the Grand Canyon phacelia, Mohave aster, twining snapdragon, Goodding verbena, climbing milkweed, purple bladderpod, trailing four o'clock, firecracker penstemon, Utah beardtongue, crimson monkeyflower, greenstem paperflower, spiny goldenweed, parry tackstem, groundcherry, desert trumpet, desert tobacco, sacred datura, sand verbena, and watercress.

CACTI

There are about 24 species of cacti found in the Grand Canyon. Noted for their amazing flowers, the blossoms of Canyon cacti are mostly red or reddish-purple, and sometimes yellow. Grand Canyon cacti also tend to be shrubby, typically forming low mats or clumps. Most of the varieties of cacti are found in the Canyon, where they grow in hot, arid places among rocks, grasses, and shrubs. Some examples you might encounter are cottontop cactus, Engelmann hedgehog cactus, California barrel cactus,

Sego Lily

fishhook cactus, beavertail cactus, and pancake pear cactus. On the rims, keep an eye out for the desert prickly pear and the grizzly bear cactus.

TREES AND SHRUBS

Hedgehog Cactus

The Grand Canyon is home to about 200 species of trees and shrubs. Although naturally insulated from temperature extremes by bark and woody branches, they still adapt to the cold by lowering the water content of their sap. The remaining sap acts like antifreeze, freezing at lower temperatures than water. The limbs of the trees and shrubs are also flexible, so they won't break under the weight of snow. You'll probably notice some bent trees on the steep canyon slopes. This is the result of the downward movement of the snowpack, which causes young trees to bend just above the base.

Along the South and North Rims, the more common trees you'll find include the ponderosa pine, Colorado pinyon, Utah juniper, and Gambel oak. On the North Rim, which has higher elevations and a cooler, wetter environment, you'll also see white fir, subalpine fir, Engelmann spruce, Douglas fir, common juniper, bigtooth maple, and quaking aspen. Some of the shrubs you may run into along both rims include the arroyo willow, Mormon tea, banana yucca, century plant, wax currant, cliff rose, Apache plume, littleleaf and true mountain mahogany, rabbitbrush, Utah serviceberry, shrubby creambush, big sagebrush, and the mock orange. Along the North Rim you'll also find the greenleaf manzanita, water birch, chokecherry, creeping barberry, and the New Mexican locust.

Below the rims, some of the trees and shrubs found primarily in the canyons include the salt-cedar or tamarisk, canyon grape, western redbud, greasebush, brittlebush, trixis, arrowweed, Fremont cottonwood, red willow, seep-willow, blackbrush, yellowleaf silktassel, catclaw acacia, honey mesquite, creosote bush, and ocotillo.

Yellow Ragweed

For further reading on the plants of the Grand Canyon, be sure to pick up a copy of *A Field Guide to the Grand Canyon* by Stephen R. Whitney.

Our hot summers and freezing winters limit the park's growing season, but throughout the Grand Canyon you will find a short but spectacular display of wildflowers at every elevation and in all types of habitats.

Generally, wildflowers in the park grow only in mild temperatures and in soil that is moist. Their growth depends entirely on the winter season; a late, wet winter means more wildflowers. A dry winter does not bode well for you flower hunters. Following germination in early spring, the development of roots and shoots is fast, with flowers and seeds produced in a few weeks, after which the plants die.

SOUTH RIM
When the warm temperatures arrive on the South Rim you'll see wildflowers in profusion along the roads and in the forests. Around the visitor center look for colorful patches of lupine, and, depending on the winter rains, the twice-blooming cliff rose. Because of the relatively mild temperatures on the higher-elevation rim, wildflowers can be seen here from spring (when they're most plentiful) through fall. Some of the more commonly seen wildflowers include baby white asters, yellow sunflowers, golden western wallflowers, orange globemallow, and rabbitbrush. In the woodland forests of the rim, look for the orange-red Indian paintbrush, the purple hill lupine, and, occasionally, a prickly pear cactus.

NORTH RIM
Spring on the North Rim is the best time to see an amazing array of shapes and colors. Some of the most impressive displays can be found along the road to Cape Royal and Point

Cliff Rose

Imperial, and in the meadows along the rim, especially those at the trailheads for the Uncle Jim and Widforss Trails. Just below the rim, in moist shady places, look for the wild strawberry and the bright red skyrocket. In sunny areas, watch for the white flowers of yarrow and the long yellow flowers of the Utah deervetch. In the meadows you'll probably see the orange mountain dandelion, and the yellow flowers of the pale mountain dandelion.

INNER CANYON

Below the rims in the Grand Canyon you'll find a mosaic of wildflowers from March until June, with some wildflowers blooming into October following the summer monsoon thunderstorms. Some of the wildflowers to look for include the blue to purple flowers of the Grand Canyon phacelia in the Inner Gorge area of the western Grand Canyon; the white or blue flowers of the Mohave aster on the talus slopes and dry places on the Canyon walls; the bright red flowers of the crimson monkeyflower in shady seeps and stream banks in the Canyon; the magenta flowers of the trailing four o'clock in the Canyon, Inner Gorge, and Tonto Platform; and the purple lobes of the twining snapdragon vine, found on shaded ledges in the Inner Gorge and the side canyons. You'll also see flowering cacti, mostly on the Canyon floor, from March until October.

Prickle Poppy

Here are some hints on what to look for as you travel around the park:

⇨ Evening primroses, on both rims, along roads, and in open areas. From May until summer, these flowers open in the evening and close in the morning sun.

⇨ The stately sego lily, the state flower of Utah, in open areas on both rims.

⇨ The Utah agave, a widespread flowering plant found at every elevation from rim to river.

⇨ Cliff rose along open areas on the South Rim, and along Bright Angel and Kaibab Trails. The white flowers are common from April to June.

⇨ Desert phlox, along the same trails, in April. The flowers vary from white to deep pink.

⇨ Prickle-poppy, which grows in many disturbed areas and begins to flower after many of the other spring flowers have gone to seed.

For more information, refer to the books listed in "Further Reading" on pages 213–214. You might also want to pick up a copy of Art Phillips's book *Grand Canyon Wildflowers*.

To tell you the truth, the Grand Canyon wouldn't be my first choice for fall color. We do have golden displays of cottonwoods along tributary streams throughout the Canyon, oaks scattered along the rims and in the side canyons, and aspens bordering meadows on the North Rim and in the higher elevations, but they're scattered in small pockets.

In the nearby areas, the best place to see fall color is outside park boundaries, along 50 miles of U.S. Highway 180, between Flagstaff and the Highway 64 junction. You can also see glorious color around the San Francisco Peaks. From late August through October, cottonwood, willow, and aspens ignite the area with gold. But watch out; by early November you could get hit by the first winter storms and road closures.

As you leave the Grand Canyon via the South Entrance Road, follow Highway 64 for 28 miles until you reach the Highway 180 turnoff. This curvy, two-lane road with lots of hills winds through Kaibab National Forest. You'll see areas of sagebrush opening to ponderosa and pinyon-juniper-aspen forests, followed by a large stand of aspen that frames the San Francisco Peaks just outside of Flagstaff. This is a distinctly volcanic landscape that gives rise to the majestic San Francisco Peaks: Humphreys Peak, at 12,643 ft. the highest point in Arizona; Kendrick Peak (10,418 ft.); Agassiz Peak (12,356 ft.); and Doyle Peak (11,969 ft.).

As you drive toward Flagstaff on U.S. Highway 180, take some time to stop and look around at the awesome landscape. There are several turnouts that provide overviews of this area and its mountains. Just pay attention to traffic, which reaches its height during the summer months. Don't forget to pick up a good road map of the South and North Kaibab National Forest, for sale at the visitor center.

Here are some other suggestions for good fall color viewing:
⇨ For spectacular views of the Kaibab Forest, visit the Snowbowl ski area at the San Francisco Peaks, and take the chair lift.
⇨ Drive along the network of forest service dirt roads that circle and traverse the San Francisco Peaks area (not recommended during wet weather).

What Indian tribe built the Desert View Watchtower?

Although it looks like it could have been built by one of the area's Native American tribes, the Watchtower was actually designed in the early 1930s by Mary Colter, architect for the Fred Harvey Company and Santa Fe Railway. She designed it as a gift shop and resting place offering dramatic views of the Canyon for the company's sightseeing tours.

Ms. Colter spent months traveling around the Southwest, studying and sketching remains of prehistoric Pueblo towers in the Four Corners. This enabled her to capture the texture and spirit of ancient Native American buildings. Colter also spent time studying the Desert View site to take advantage of every detail of the panoramic view, and to design a structure that fit with the surrounding landforms and landscape.

Once she determined the precise location for the building, she had the Santa Fe Railway build a 70-foot-high metal and wood scaffolding. It became the highest point on the South Rim, with 360-degree views of the Painted Desert, San Francisco Peaks, Vermilion Cliffs, and beyond.

Stones for the exterior were gathered from the local area, and interior furnishings were handcrafted from tree trunks and wood burls of local species. Colter hired local Hopi artist Fred Kabotie to paint a tribal mural in the ceremonial room, or kiva. In the center of the room is a beautiful sand painting of a Hopi Indian Snake altar.

Since the building opened in 1933, the Watchtower at Desert View has been a favorite place for both visitors and locals to capture the spectacular vistas of the Canyon.

For more information on Mary Colter, refer to pages 184–185 in Quick Reference or pick up a copy of *Mary Colter: Builder Upon the Red Earth* by Virginia Graton.

Mary Colter
Photo courtesy Grand Canyon
National Park Museum Collection,
#16950

Although we don't know very much about their lives, we know that humans have been a part of the Grand Canyon region for at least 4,000 years. A major clue comes in the form of hundreds of mysterious stick figures found in limestone caves high on the Canyon walls. Because the stick figures resemble animals, including some stuck with a small spear and placed in shrine-like formations, most archaeologists think they were good luck totems for hunters.

Where did these people come from? If we go back in time about 12,000 years, we learn that people crossed Russia's Siberian peninsula to Alaska in North America during the Ice Age. Many of these ancient people ventured southward into the United States, Mexico, and South America. Artifact dating tells us that people probably lived in or around the Grand Canyon for at least part of the year, leaving the stick figures made from twigs of willow and cottonwood in the caves, and giving us a vital link to the past.

Split-twig figurine from willow. 4,000 years old. Similar to others found in Canyon caves.

About 1,500 years ago, the ancestral Pueblo people, sometimes known as the Anasazi (ancient ones) arrived in the region now known as the Colorado Plateau, and began living in and around the Grand Canyon. These people excelled in handicrafts, perfecting basketry and the manufacture of other functional items like sandals, bags, and clothing. For cold weather, they interlaced rabbit fur or deerskin strips to make capes and blankets. They also made beautiful ceramic bowls, ladles, jars, pitchers, and even canteens.

For a constant source of meat, the ancestral Pueblo people tamed and kept wild turkeys. They also hunted deer, antelope, and bighorn sheep, and gathered pinyon nuts, yucca pods, and cactus fruits. Their skills in the field resulted in small, controlled crops of corn, beans, and squash. They even developed irrigation systems using water collected from rains on the Colorado Plateau.

Skilled and prolific builders, the ancestral Pueblo people constructed cliff dwellings of mud and stone. Later, more intricate structures were sometimes built several stories high, called *pueblos* (from the Spanish word meaning "village"). Without the help of horses, which would arrive in the fifteenth century, they built pueblos in areas that now include parts of the South and North Rims, and the bottom of the Canyon by the Colorado River.

South Rim. Although more than 2,700 prehistoric Pueblo sites have been discovered in the Grand Canyon region, most are far from any roads and trails. Some are located on the tops of plateaus that were once part of the Canyon's rims, but are now isolated "islands" in the desert, like the Powell Plateau seen from Pima and Hopi Point on the South Rim. One carefully excavated site, Tusayan, is located just a few miles east of Grand Canyon Village on the South Rim, and is accessible by road. A visit here reveals glimpses of what life must have been like for a hamlet of about thirty ancestral Pueblo people, who lived here for about twenty years during the late twelfth century. A self-guided walking tour of the site takes roughly one hour to complete. The site consists of an open plaza in the middle of a U-shaped pueblo where the villagers did their crafts, prepared their food, and played many games, including racing, throwing, dolls, tops, darts, singing, and gambling. The people cooked, ate, and slept in second-story rooms with storage rooms along each side. Close by the plaza was a round, sunken structure known as a kiva, which was used as a

"Descending Sheep" petroglyph panes (detail), up Colorado River from Lees Ferry
Photo courtesy Grand Canyon National Park Museum Collection, # 6185

"Descending Sheep" petroglyph panes (detail), up Colorado River from Lees Ferry
Photo courtesy Grand Canyon National Park Museum Collection, # 6185

village gathering place and ceremonial center. They enjoyed wearing fine jewelry and clothing, which they probably secured from neighboring villages by trading their beautiful baskets and pottery.

Inner Canyon. Inside the Canyon below Lipan Point, the Unkar Delta is the site of numerous ancestral Pueblo dwellings dating from the ninth to the early twelfth century. Life along this area of alluvial terraces focused on farming, with early living sites built on the fertile terraces along Unkar Creek. As the population grew, living sites were moved to the slopes above the creek to make room for more crops. During the summer months, farming was probably done on the Canyon's cooler, moister North Rim (Walhalla Glades) rather than the Unkar Delta. There is a self-guided loop trail that can be accessed by a trip on the river beginning at Lees Ferry. This tour through the past explores thirteen individual family living and storage sites, as well as several larger pueblos above and along Unkar Creek.

North Rim. On the North Rim, the Walhalla Glades site was the summer home of a small farming village of about twenty people, who grew corn, beans, and squash, and returned to the Canyon (probably to Unkar Delta) in winter. A "peninsula" surrounded on three sides by the Grand Canyon, Walhalla Glades has a lower elevation than most of the North Rim, allowing updrafts of warm air from the Canyon to melt winter snows early. This made it a perfect spot for farming. Access is along the road to Cape Royal, with a one-mile hike down the Cliff Spring Trail. More than one hundred farm sites have been found on Walhalla Glades, most with a one-room field house and agricultural terraces or garden plots. The site contains an ancestral Pueblo dwelling with nine rooms used for sleeping, eating, and storage. Additional food storage and processing was done in the Sky Island area, which is visible from the Walhalla Overlook. A good example of a granary storage room can be seen as you walk down the Cliff Springs Trail. There is a self-guided walking tour available at the site.

During the late twelfth and early thirteenth centuries, the American Southwest suffered a series of droughts. The land could no longer support the agricultural demands of farming and a growing population. Eventually, the ancestral Pueblo people abandoned their villages and migrated south and east to the Hopi Mesas and the Rio Grande River Valley. Their culture evolved to become the modern-day Pueblo people—the Hopi and Pueblos of the Rio Grande Valley in New Mexico.

For more information on ancestral Pueblo culture, visit the Tusayan Ruins and Museum, or call the museum at (520) 638-2305.

"Descending Sheep" petroglyph panes (detail), up Colorado River from Lees Ferry
Photo courtesy Grand Canyon National Park Museum Collection, # 6185

When did the first Euro-Americans come to Grand Canyon?

The year was 1540—Spaniard Francisco Vásquez de Coronado was leading a search for the mythic Seven Cities of Cibola in the southwestern United States. He sent a party northward under the command of García López de Cárdenas, whose small troop became the first Europeans to set eyes on the Grand Canyon. Their search for riches, however, proved futile, as they were unable to find a way across the great void of the canyon, thereby failing to find a valuable land or water route. They returned to Mexico with tales of a great canyon, with an unreachable river at its bottom.

The late 1500s saw the return of the Spanish to the region, not as explorers, but as colonists. By 1776, efforts were in full swing to convert the native peoples to Christianity and to extract tributes for the Spanish kingdom. One of these missionaries, Francisco Thomas Garces, traveling with native guides, reached the crimson cliffs of the western Grand Canyon near the outlet of Havasu Creek on the North Rim. After spending six days with the Havasupai, he followed a high and narrow cliff trail to a plateau covered with pinyon and juniper. There, he saw his first view of the Grand Canyon.

By the early 1800s, trappers and traders discovered that beavers were plentiful in Spanish-governed "New Spain" (Mexico, Arizona, New Mexico, California, Colorado, Utah). More opportunists flooded the area in 1821, with the opening of the Santa Fe Trail and its east-west trade routes. In 1848, much of the Southwest came under U.S. control after the war with Mexico. The U.S. government sent out teams of engineers to survey the new territories. One party leader, Lieutenant Joseph Christmas Ives, wrote, "Ours has been the first, and will doubtless be the last, party of whites to visit this profitless locality." Needless to say, his words were not prophetic!

In 1869 John Wesley Powell, a one-armed Civil War veteran, led a team of four wooden boats and ten

John Wesley Powell
Photo courtesy Grand Canyon National Park Museum Collection

men on a 1,000-mile Colorado River trip that went through the Canyon—the first Euro-Americans to make the journey. His expeditions, and recent efforts to preserve natural resources and Native American rights, greatly influenced the future of the region.

That future proved to be a boom of visitors, homesteaders, and miners in the late 1800s. While geographers, artists, naturalists, photographers, and writers spread the word about a canyon "without rival upon the face of the globe," entrepreneurs were finding their niches. One homesteader was the infamous John D. Lee, a Mormon sent by the church to start the first ferry service across the upper Colorado River. Today, all river runners put in at Lees Ferry.

A slew of miners came to the Grand Canyon looking for profitable zinc, copper, lead, and asbestos mining claims; they included men like Cass Hite, John Hance, William Wallace Bass, Peter D. Berry, the Cameron brothers, Louis Boucher, and Daniel L. Hogan. Even though these mines never amounted to much, the prospectors soon found themselves tapping a different kind of resource: tourists.

Tau-Gu, Chief of the Paiutes, overlooking
Virgin River with J. W. Powell
Photo courtesy Grand Canyon National Park Museum Collection, #17229

61

Are there historic buildings in Grand Canyon National Park?

There are a number of interesting historic structures along both rims and even down in the canyon itself, but most of them are located right in Grand Canyon Village. We've provided a walking map that reads from left to right, or west to east. All of the buildings described here are included in the Grand Canyon Historic District and are listed in the National Register of Historic Places.

1. Red Horse Station, built in the 1890s and originally located 16 miles away, was relocated to its present site in 1902 by Ralph Cameron. At that point it was renamed Cameron's Hotel and Camp. It served for a number of years as the terminus of the Flagstaff-to-Grand Canyon stage run, and also as the village post office.

2. Kolb Studio. Between 1904 and 1926, the brothers Kolb—Ellsworth and Emery—built, altered, and added to this building. The brothers felt that there was a market among visitors for scenic photographs of the Canyon, so they set up a photographic studio and photographed thousands of mule-ride passengers as they began their descent into the Canyon. When riders returned several hours later, their portraits were ready for purchase. Today, prints of these photographs are available from the University of Northern Arizona Library.

3. Lookout Studio, located on the edge of the Grand Canyon rim, was designed by architect Mary Colter to resemble the stone structures built by Southwest Indians. The structure was built of native stone in 1914, providing a lounge and fireplace, as well as a room where postcards and

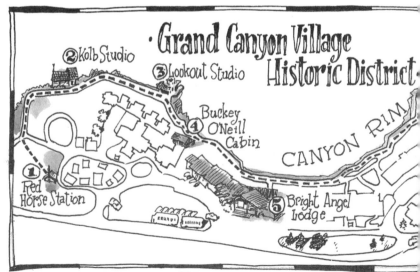

artwork could be purchased. Outside on the porch was a powerful telescope that allowed visitors to study details of the Canyon.

4. Buckey O'Neill's Cabin, built in the 1890s, is the oldest structure on the Canyon rim, and was the cabin of one of the Grand Canyon's most colorful characters. Buckey O'Neill was a prospector, politician, writer, lawman, and mayor of Prescott, Arizona. He served as a Rough Rider in the Spanish-American War with Teddy Roosevelt. He was killed the day before the famous charge up San Juan Hill.

5. Bright Angel Lodge, another Mary Colter design, opened for business in 1935 to provide housing for budget-minded visitors. They could stay either in the lodge itself or in one of the cabins that cluster to the west of the lodge. Be sure to see the lounge's stone fireplace, which reflects the geologic strata of the Canyon, from the Kaibab limestone at the Canyon's rim, down to the river-worn stones at the bottom.

6. El Tovar Hotel is a 1905 masterpiece of a log-built structure that was designed by architect Charles Whittlesey for the Santa Fe Railroad, which had just begun regular train service from Flagstaff to the Canyon. In its early days, the El Tovar sported a barbershop, music room, solarium, bar, art room, and dining room.

7. Hopi House was also completed in 1905. Again, it was designed by Mary Colter, but in this case, most of the actual construction was done by Hopi Indians. After it was completed, a number of the Hopi lived in the building, creating rugs, basketry, and silver jewelry, and giving visitors a glimpse of native culture.

8. Verkamp's Curios is an offshoot of what was originally a souvenir shop operated by John Verkamp in 1898. In 1905, a big construction year in the village, he built his curio shop, and for many years after, the Verkamp family lived above the store. Today it is operated by Michael Verkamp, grandson of the store's founder.

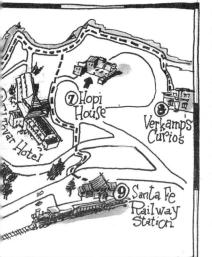

9. Santa Fe Railway Station, completed in 1909, is one of only three log-constructed railway stations still in existence in the United States. The architect was Francis Wilson, and of his many commissions, this was his only log structure. Today, the station is the terminus for the Grand Canyon Railway, whose daily service was reinstated in the 1980s by Max and Thelma Biegert.

For additional reading, see *A Guide to the Grand Canyon Village Historic District* by Timothy Manns.

What role did the Army and the Civilian Conservation Corps play in Grand Canyon's history?

During the late 1840s, soldiers were some of the most adventuresome explorers of the Grand Canyon area. But it was a secondary role the army played—that of overseeing and paying for the Civilian Conservation Corps (CCC) camps in the 1930s—that helped transform the "big canyon" into the Grand Canyon that we know today.

The CCC, created by President Franklin D. Roosevelt in April, 1933, was the first of the New Deal agencies, and Roosevelt's favorite. Its mission was to accomplish simple work (not interfering with normal employment) confined to forestry, the prevention of soil erosion, flood control, and similar projects that conserved and developed the nation's natural resources. Roosevelt wrote, "This enterprise will pay dividends to the present and future generations. It will make improvements in national and state domains which have been largely forgotten in the

Construction of River Trail by CCC enrollees
Photo courtesy Grand Canyon National Park Museum Collection, #3973c

past few years of industrial development.... More important, however, than the material gains will be the moral and spiritual value of such work." By the end of the CCC's eight years of operation, almost three million people had been put to work, at a total cost of $634 million.

Between 1933 and 1942, five companies of CCC workers (about 1,000 men) virtually transformed Grand Canyon National Park. During their tenure in the park, the CCC built or improved parts of the South Kaibab and Bright Angel Trails; most of Phantom Ranch; the Mile-and-a-Half, Three-Mile, Indian Garden, and Pipe Creek rest houses along the Bright Angel Trail; and the masonry walls that border all the lookout points and scenic turnouts. The CCC also was responsible for upgrading and maintaining trails throughout the park; building service roads; building the first trans-canyon telephone line; landscaping; cleaning ditches; and assembling service structures and cattle fences.

For many it was a labor of love, the benefits of which can still be found today in Grand Canyon National Park. For more information on the CCC at the Grand Canyon, pick up a copy of *The Ace in the Hole: A Brief History of Company 818 of the Civilian Conservation Corps* by Louis Lester Purvis.

THE GRAND CANYON RAILWAY

On September 17, 1901, the first passenger train arrived at the South Rim via the Santa Fe Grand Canyon Railway. The rail line served for many years as a popular way to travel to the Canyon. The beautiful Grand Canyon Depot was completed in 1910 and served as the arrival and departure point for all trains.

The heyday of this elegant way of travel faded as the popularity of the automobile grew, and in 1968 passenger train service to the Grand Canyon ceased. For many years the railbed sat unused and the depot fell into decay. Then in 1987 Max and Thelma Biegert, who were in the aviation business, collected the collateral on a delinquent loan: 22 miles of steel railroad track, part of the long-defunct Santa Fe Grand Canyon rail line. They decided to try to reintroduce rail service to the Canyon. They acquired rail cars and two vintage steam engines and soon were running passenger train service to the Canyon again from the Williams depot. By 1993 they were carrying over 100,000 passengers to the Canyon and back each year, eliminating approximately 40,000 auto trips to the park. The hour-and-a-half, one-way trip from Williams to the Canyon covers 65 miles of scenic western landscape at 40 mph or less. The 1910 depot is now a National Historic Landmark, and is still used to greet trains arriving at the Canyon today.

Oil-burning vintage steam engines operate from Memorial Day Weekend to the end of September, and vintage diesel locomotives pull the train the remainder of the year. Daily service is available except Christmas Eve and Christmas day. A variety of fares and accommodations are available, with round-trip coach fares starting at $49.50 for adults and $19.50 for children (16 and under).

For full details about train and hotel reservations via Grand Canyon Railway, call (800) 843-8724. International callers should call (520) 773-1976. Information is also available on their website at www.thetrain.com.

September 17, 1901: the first scheduled passenger train arrived at the Canyon from Williams, Arizona
Photo courtesy Grand Canyon National Park Museum Collection, #2435

What can I take home as a memento of my visit?

With an awe-inspiring backdrop like the Grand Canyon, anyone with a camera can take home some of the magic without stealing anything away from the beauty of the park. There are no mementos quite like the photographs that capture your own special memories, such as a dip in the pools in front of Havasu Falls, a walk through a meadow of wildflowers near Uncle Jim Trail, or a view of the sunrise from Imperial Point.

For less personal keepsakes, check out the park shops, galleries, and museums. Besides the ever-popular t-shirts and mugs, there is a wide range of gifts that evoke the spirit of the Grand Canyon. These include hand-wrought gold and silver jewelry made by world-renowned Indian artists from the Hopi, Zuni, Navajo, and Santa Domingo tribes; basketry crafted by Hopi, Paiute, Navajo, and Papago artisans; Hopi carved Kachina Dolls; Navajo rugs; minerals, petrified wood, and fossils; authentic Indian pottery; moccasins, jackets and leather goods; and paintings of the Grand Canyon that range in price from $300 to $1,800.

The search for natural souvenirs can become a problem in the Grand Canyon. That's why people are prohibited from destroying or removing just about everything in the park, including plants, driftwood, animals, antlers, minerals, and especially any archaeological artifacts. The Canyon's fragile archaeological resources provide important and tangible links to the area's history, and must remain a part of the park's archaeological record. That's why a family driving out of the Canyon with a pile of rocks shouldn't be surprised if the ranger hands over a $50–$100 citation—one of the less desirable of Grand Canyon mementos. These regulations are designed to keep the Canyon intact, despite the nearly five million visitors per year who want to take a piece of it home.

Getting Around

AIR TOURS ◀

SHUTTLE BUS STOP ▶

◀ MOTORCOACH TOURS

BICYCLE RENTAL ▶

◀ HIKING TRAILS

PARK AUTO ROUTES ▶

◀ TAXI SERVICE

MULE RIDES ▶

◀ RIVER TRIPS

NATURE STUDY TRIPS ▶

◀ • WINTER • CROSS-COUNTRY SKIING SNOWSHOEING

Decisions.. Decisions..

What's the best way to see the park?

There are so many ways to see and enjoy the Grand Canyon, you might want to take several modes of transportation during your stay in the park. Here's a sampling of your options.

Walking

Year-round, the best way to escape the crowds and see the Grand Canyon is to hoof it—walking, hiking, or backpacking some of the more than 33 miles of maintained trails within the park boundaries. You can take these trails along the Rims or down into the Canyon. Hikes range from easy walks along the North and South Rims to view the Canyon from scenic lookout points, to steeper treks into the Canyon and remote backcountry areas. Remember that even the relatively flat Rim Trail along Hermit Road, which is paved between Yavapai Point and Maricopa Point, and unpaved on to Hermits Rest, can be dangerous—especially near the cliff edges. And, although the scenic viewpoints have guard rails, they're not childproof. You'll need to assess your limits before setting out on one of the Inner Canyon journeys. Don't forget to bring lots of water, snacks, and extra clothes in case of a sudden change in weather. The Grand Canyon is desert country, with intense heat during the summer. Read up on backcountry regulations and safety. Take a look at pages 132–135 to find out about some great day hikes. It's a good idea to stop at the nearest visitor center or ranger station for an update on trail closures and conditions before you start.

Shuttle Bus

(times are approximate). Year-round, the park provides a free shuttle service for visitors on the South Rim, with no tickets required. Taking the shuttle with a few short walks is a great way to view the Canyon and enjoy the scenery along the way. Currently, the shuttle follows three loop routes: one in the Grand Canyon Village, one on Hermit Road (formerly West Rim Drive), and one on Desert View Drive (formerly East Rim Drive) to Yaki Point and South Kaibab Trailhead. These routes may change once the Canyon View Information Plaza opens in the fall, 2000. The shuttle makes frequent stops that are clearly marked along the way. Beginning in late 2000, there will be continuous shuttle service from the new Canyon View Transportation Hub. Times of operation for this new continuous shuttle service will be found in *The Guide*. Currently, the West Rim Loop shuttle departs daily every 15 minutes from 7:30 a.m. until just before sunset. This route goes from the West Rim Interchange towards Hermits Rest, with stops at eight scenic overlooks along the way. On the return trip, the shuttle only stops at Mohave and Hopi Points. Although this isn't a tour, if you want to stay on the bus for the entire loop, you should plan on 90 minutes. The Village Loop shuttle runs daily every 15 minutes between 6:30 a.m. and 9:45 p.m. This route travels between the Yavapai Observation Station, South Rim Visitor Center, hotels, restaurants, campgrounds, and other facilities in the Village area (see map on page 25). Allow 50 minutes to travel the entire loop without getting off the bus. The Yaki Point/South Kaibab Loop shuttle runs every 30 minutes from one hour before sunrise until one hour after sunset. This route goes between Bright Angel Lodge, Maswik Transportation Center (Backcountry Office), and Yavapai Lodge. Check *The Guide* for pick-up and drop-off times at each stop. There is no shuttle to Desert View, nor is there a shuttle on the North Rim of the Grand Canyon.

Taxi When the Yaki Point/South Kaibab shuttle is not in operation, taxi service is available on the South Rim by calling (520) 638-2631, ext. 6563 or (520) 638-2822. The cost is $8 for the first person, and $3 for each additional person. No taxi service is available on the North Rim.

Driving Starting in early 2000, Hermit Road and the Yaki Point/South Kaibab Trailhead road will have restrictions for private and commercial vehicles. During our peak season (April–October), you will be sharing our limited driving roads with lots of other traffic. You'll also be competing for parking spaces, which is often the most challenging part of any visit to the Canyon during peak times. When you can, take the shuttle to avoid parking headaches. You can also purchase a mile-by-mile, annotated road guide containing detailed information about all park roads, as well as information about places to go and things to see as you drive. These road guides are available for as little as $6.95 at visitor and information centers or in Grand Canyon Association bookstores. Both Rims of the Canyon experience storms and freezing temperatures. Summer thunderstorms may be brief, but they can make driving dangerous, with fierce hail and lightning. It's a good idea to call (520) 779-2711 for current road information before you arrive at the park.

Bicycling

You can bike all of the paved roads open to private vehicles, plus the restricted Hermit Road, but beware of motorists who may not be aware of you. Biking here is not for novice riders. You need to be in good shape and pay close attention to auto traffic, because shoulders are narrow to non-existent along roadways. Bicycles are not allowed on any park trails, and bicyclists must obey all traffic regulations in the park. They should always ride with the flow of traffic. In the winter, snow and narrower roads create challenging biking conditions, while spring and fall are the best times for riding. Consider riding at first light to avoid heavy traffic and hot temperatures. The closest bicycle rentals, parts, and repairs are available in the towns of Flagstaff and Sedona, Arizona, north of the park. See page 207 in "Quick Reference" for a list of places that can help you with your bicycling needs.

Motorcoach Tours

Narrated motorcoach tours of the South Rim are available year-round via Fred Harvey Company buses ("Harveycars"). These tours include trips along Hermit Road to Hermits Rest (2 hours), Desert View Drive to Desert View (4 hours), or a combination Grand Tour along both roads. For spectacular views of the sun rising and setting over the Canyon, take a Sunrise & Sunset Tour, which stops at various scenic lookouts along Hermit Road. From November to March, the Sunset tour becomes part of the Hermits Rest tour. Prices are as follows: Hermits Rest ($14.50/person), Desert View ($25.50/person), Grand Tour ($30.50/person), and Sunrise & Sunset ($11; kids 16 and under free). Call Grand Canyon National Park Lodges for more information at (520) 638-2631 or (303) 29-PARKS. There are no concessionaire-operated motorcoach tours of the North Rim. The Grand Canyon Railway (see page 65) also offers narrated motorcoach tours along Hermit Road and Desert View Drive, in combination with the Grand Canyon Railway train trip from Williams, Arizona, to the South Rim of the Canyon. There are several tours you can choose from, including the Grand Tour (3 hours, lunch in Arizona Room, $34/adult, $25/children 16 & under); the Special Tour (3 hours, buffet lunch at Maswik Lodge, $26/adult, $20/children 16 & under); and the Freedom Tour (1½ hours, box lunch, $23/adult, $18/children 16 & under). These tours depart from the Grand Canyon train depot upon the train's arrival at the South Rim, and return you to the depot for the return trip to Williams. You can also take a railroad Express Tour, which combines travel by bus (Harveycar) to Williams and return to the Canyon by historic train, or vice versa. For reservations and more information, call the Grand Canyon Railway at (800) 843-8724, or visit their website at www.thetrain.com. International callers use (520) 773-1976. For commercial bus tours or service to the Grand Canyon, call Gray Line of Flagstaff (run by Nava-Hopi Tours) at (800) 892-8687, South Rim Travel at (888) 291-9116, or contact your travel agent.

Mule & Horseback Trips, Wagon Rides

On the South Rim, you can saddle up a horse or mule for a one-hour ($25) or two-hour ($40) guided ride through the forests of Kaibab National Forest. Or, you can take a four-hour ($65) guided ride through Long Jim Canyon. These rides depart daily from Moqui Lodge (Apache Stables), just outside the south entrance station to the park. There are also twilight campfire rides through the Kaibab National Forest on horseback ($30), or rides in a horse-drawn wagon ($8.50). For more information and reservations call (520) 638-2891 or (520) 638-2424, or visit the website at www.apachestables.com. Grand Canyon National Park Lodges also offer a one-day mule trip below the South Rim in the Canyon. The seven-hour trip descends to Plateau Point along the Bright Angel Trail, and includes lunch. You can also book an overnight mule trip to Phantom Ranch, including box lunch and accommodations at the Ranch. The cost for the one-day Plateau Point trip is $106.60/person, and $295–$523 for the Phantom Ranch overnight trip. During the winter months, there is a three-day/two-night trip to Phantom Ranch available. Rider restrictions apply for all trips. For more information and reservations, call (303) 29-PARKS. Along the North Rim you have several mule trips to choose from, including a one-hour Rim Ride ($15), a half-day ride to Uncle Jim's Point ($35), a half-day trip to Supai Tunnel in the Canyon ($35), or a one-day trip to Roaring Springs in the Canyon ($85). For more information and reservations, call Canyon Trail Rides at (435) 679-8665. There are also multi-day horseback trips into the Grand Canyon backcountry outside park boundaries with experienced guides. Call (435) 644-8150 for more information.

River Trips

There are half-day and full-day excursions that provide visitors with a leisurely day rafting on the Colorado River and enjoying a picnic lunch on a beach in Glen Canyon. You embark at Glen Canyon Dam, raft 15 miles of the river from Glen Canyon Dam to Lees Ferry, and board a bus at Lees Ferry for the trip back to the

Dam, arriving at approximately 7:00 p.m. For more information, call (800) 528-6154; (520) 645-3279; or (520) 638-2424. For longer trips on the river, you can contact one of the many commercial concessionaires who guide all levels of river trips down the Colorado. Refer to the outfitters list on pages 191–192.

Air Tours

If you want to take to the sky to see the Grand Canyon, you have several choices. For a list of fixed-wing and helicopter tour operators, refer to page 206 in "Quick Reference."

Cross-country Skiing & Snowshoeing

During the winter (November–March), the national forest lands around the park offer limited backcountry trails for cross-country skiers and snowshoers. On the South Rim, you can ski around the Kaibab National Forest, where you may find groomed trails near Grandview Point. Call the Tusayan Ranger Station at (520) 638-2443 for more information. On the North Rim, you can again try Kaibab National Forest lands. You may even be able to ski to park boundaries on the Jacob Lake Road once it's closed for the season. For more information, call the North Kaibab Ranger Station at (520) 643-7395.

Nature Study Trips & Field Courses

The Grand Canyon Field Institute offers year-round short field courses on all aspects of life at the Grand Canyon. Activities range from classroom presentations to hiking, horsepacking, and river-rafting and river-running in the park. Most courses last from two to five days, with tuition varying from $95 for hiking and journal-keeping in the Grand Canyon, to $975 for llama-trekking in a remote corner of the North Rim. For more information, call the Grand Canyon Field Institute at (520) 638-2485.

What do we need to know about the shuttle along the South Rim?

First of all, you need to make sure that you get on the bus that's going to your desired destination. That's easy; currently, all you have to do is read the name on the front of each brown-and-tan, or white-with-green-stripes, bus. The name will indicate one of the following routes: West Rim, Village, or Yaki Point/South Kaibab. For a map of the South Rim shuttles, see page 22. Don't worry if you "just" missed a shuttle bus; another one will be coming by your stop soon. Enjoy the scenery while you wait. This may change somewhat after the Canyon View Information Plaza opens in late 2000. Check *The Guide* for the latest information.

It's important to know the rules for riding the shuttles. Pets are not allowed on the buses, except for service animals for visitors with disabilities. Most shuttle buses are not wheelchair-accessible. An accessibility permit is available for private vehicle use in any shuttle-only area. Ask at the visitor center about this permit. To reserve a wheelchair-accessible shuttle, you need to make arrangements at least 48 hours in advance by calling (520) 774-1697.

Lastly, some words of advice to shuttle riders. Water is not available along the West Rim, except at the last stop, Hermits Rest. It's a good idea to take a canteen or water bottle. In addition, we have thunder and lightning storms which can be a hazard. My advice is to stay away from exposed rim areas, like the lookout points, during our storms. You should always be prepared for a sudden rainstorm, especially during the summer. Take a raincoat or poncho with you on the shuttle. Finally, if you decide to walk between some of the shuttle stops (a great idea), remember to walk only along the Rim Trail. Our shuttles take up most of the road, leaving little room for pedestrians. Don't forget, there is no shuttle along the North Rim—you're on your own there.

Where are the East and West Rim Drives?

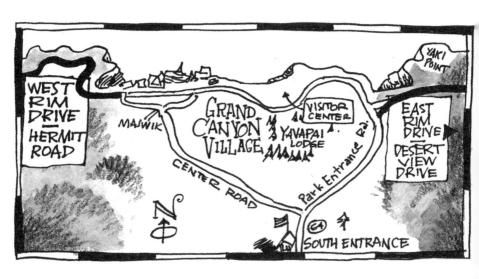

Throughout this book we have referred to the South and North Rims of the Grand Canyon. When we refer to the East and West Rims, that doesn't mean that the Canyon is square. The explanation is simple. There's a road that runs along the South Rim of the Canyon, and it runs in an east/west direction from Desert View to Hermits Rest. This rim road intersects with the south entrance road at Grand Canyon Village. Desert View Drive (or, as it was previously known, East Rim Drive) is the road from Desert View, at the east end of the rim road, west to the intersection with the south entrance road. Hermit Road (or West Rim Drive) runs from the West Rim Interchange near the Bright Angel Lodge to Hermits Rest; this is the westernmost point accessible by paved road on the South Rim. Separating the two roads is the community known as Grand Canyon Village.

Can we drive to most sights?

Yes and no. It depends on what area of the park you're exploring. Let's take a look at both Rims of the Canyon for the answers.

South Rim. Yes, you can drive to the parking areas of most lookouts on the East Rim, including Grandview Point and trailhead, Moran Point, Lipan Point, Navajo Point, and Desert View. Most lookouts do require easy walks, some longer than others. No, you can't drive to the South Kaibab Trailhead and Yaki Point off Desert View Drive (formerly East Rim Drive), because they're closed to commercial and private vehicles.

As of late 2000, you also may not be able to drive to the scenic lookouts along Hermit Road (formerly West Rim Drive). Instead, you can take the free shuttle that operates year-round from the Canyon View Information Plaza. And, although you may be able to see the Rim Trail around the hotels and restaurants in Grand Canyon Village, you can't actually drive along it. The only way to see this three-mile stretch of the South Rim is to hoof it. You might want to start or end this jaunt at one of the many eating spots along the Rim Trail. Parking will be your only headache.

North Rim. Yes, from May 15 to the first snow (usually late October to mid-November) you can drive to many viewpoints on the North Rim, including the Grand Canyon Lodge, Point Imperial, Cape Royal, Vista Encantadora, Walhalla Overlook, and the Indian Country exhibit and lookout. Two of the most spectacular vistas along this Rim, Bright Angel Point and Angel's Window, require quarter-mile walks that are relatively easy, but may seem more difficult because of the higher elevation of the North Rim.

No, you can't drive to anyplace on the North Rim beginning with the first snow. That's because the average precipitation (much of it snowfall) on the North Rim is about 26 inches annually.

Keep in mind that the park occupies an area about the size of the state of Delaware. Much of this area is roadless, but there are unmaintained dirt roads. Before venturing on any of these roads, check at the nearest ranger station or information office. Many cross restricted lands.

How can we get from the South to the North rim?

By Automobile. Even though it's a mere ten miles across the Canyon as the raven flies, the drive between the North and South Rims takes about five hours (220 miles). The roads that connect the South with the North Rim include U.S. Highways 64, 89, and 89A. Most of this drive is on a two-lane road with heavy traffic through the Navajo Indian Reservation. As the road descends from the South Rim east to Cameron, the landscape changes from woodland to blackbrush. You'll pass the Little Colorado River Overlook about 20 miles east of the park's east entrance. There is a spectacular view beyond the group of curio shops. The road is narrow and slippery when wet, but you can walk to the viewpoint. As you head north from Cameron, Highway 89 skirts the western edge of the Painted Desert, and then follows the base of the Echo Cliffs for 60 miles. At Bitter Springs you'll get onto Highway 89A to Navajo Bridge, which crosses the Colorado River. Be sure to stop at the parking area on the north side and walk out onto the old bridge for a great view of Marble Canyon. The road then skirts the base of the Vermilion Cliffs for about 25 miles. Look for soaring condors. At House Rock, you'll begin to gain altitude, as the road rises into a large ponderosa pine forest. At Jacob Lake, Highway 67 goes 32 miles south, to the boundary of the North Rim of the Grand Canyon. You'll be able to find food, fuel, and lodging at both Cameron and Jacob Lake, and precious little in-between. Because this route can be icy and snowpacked in the winter, it's best to call ahead for road conditions at (520) 779-2711 (Arizona), and (520) 638-7888 (Grand Canyon).

By Transcanyon Shuttle. Between mid-May and mid-October, there is a transcanyon shuttle service that provides daily transportation between the South and the North Rims. The shuttle bus leaves the North Rim at 7:00 a.m. and arrives at the South Rim at noon. It departs the South Rim at 1:30 p.m. and arrives at the North Rim at 6:30 p.m. Cost is $60/one way, and $100/round trip, with special rates for ten or more people. To make a reservation (required), call (520) 638-2820, or contact one of the lodging transportation desks.

By Hiking. There are a few hearty souls who actually hike across the Canyon from Rim to Rim. It's a strenuous, three-day, 21-mile trek along the North and South Kaibab Trails, and requires top physical conditioning and stamina. At one point, the trail crosses the Colorado River via a narrow footbridge 70 feet above the water. For obvious reasons, this hike is not meant for most visitors.

Why are there "School Zone" signs in the South Rim Village?

That's because the Grand Canyon is the only national park in the country to have a kindergarten–twelfth-grade school system (the graduating class usually has about 20 students). Actually, we have an entire community of year-round residents in the South Rim area, who help keep the park running all year long.

The Grand Canyon School serves about 380 students. These students are from the families of National Park Service staff, concession workers, and other personnel who call the Grand Canyon home. During weekday school hours (Monday–Thursday, 7:55 a.m.–4:15 p.m.), it's not unusual to see yellow school buses driving the roads throughout the South Rim, picking up or dropping off students near their homes. There's even a summer school that usually runs the first six weeks of summer vacation. Even though we're in a national park, all driving rules apply for our school buses, as they would in any other part of the country. If a school bus is stopped in front of you or has its lights flashing, do not attempt to pass. In front of the school, between the south entrance road and Grand Canyon Village on the South Rim, you must obey the 15-miles-per-hour speed limit when school is in session.

In addition to a school system, we also have services for our year-round residents as well as visitors, including a clinic and pharmacy, a dentist, a general store, a bank, a post office, an auto repair shop, child care services, and a radio station (KSGC 92.1 FM). Yep, it's a regular ol' little town, with about 1200 residents in peak season.

How long does it take to see the entire park?

How much time you g⟩

That's a tricky question. Some visitors say that they saw the entire park in three days (it's possible). For others, it takes a lifetime to really know the park—and even then it has surprises. The best advice I can give on the subject is to read up on the Grand Canyon, and then decide what you want to see in the amount of time you have. But, don't rush your visit here. You have to take into account the rough and unforgiving terrain, the exhausting heat of our summer months, and the amount of traffic and visitors you'll encounter during your visit to the park. Here are some of my suggestions on ways to see the park in the amount of time you have. (If you only have one day, refer to pages 20–22.

Two Days. If you have two days to spend at the Grand Canyon, I would suggest staying on the South Rim. You can begin your visit by touring the West and East Rims (by shuttle, by Harveycar tour, or by combining these with a few walks along the Rim Trail). You can add to your knowledge of this place by taking a walking tour of the buildings in the historic district of Grand Canyon Village, visiting the Tusayan Museum and Ruin along Desert View (East Rim) Drive, or joining a ranger-led walk or talk. If you feel up to it, you could take a short hike into the Canyon along the Bright Angel or South Kaibab Trails, or a longer (six-hour) mule ride to Plateau Point in the Canyon. Don't forget to enjoy the many dining options along the Rim, including breakfast at the El Tovar Hotel and dinner at the Arizona Room near the Bright Angel Lodge. To make your South Rim excursion a really memorable one, make sure you watch a sunrise or sunset over the Canyon. Then, on your next visit to the Grand Canyon, you can explore the North Rim.

WAKE UP! LET'S CATCH THE SUNRISE!

zzzzz

WHAT SAY WE CATCH THE SUNSET?

Three Days. If you have three days to spend, and you want to see both the North and South Rims, then you'll have to pick from the South Rim activities above so that they fit into one-and-a-half days. Be

sure you have advance room reservations or a campsite reserved at the Jacob Lake Campground. Then, you can drive to the North Rim (five hours straight through), making stops to see Desert View, Cameron, the Navajo Indian Reservation, Lees Ferry, and many scenic areas along the way. With stops, the drive could take you six to seven hours. That will leave you one day to see the North Rim. You can spend some time touring the Rim by taking a short walk to Bright Angel Point and other easy access trails, including Cliff Springs and Cape Royal. You can take a drive along the Cape Royal Road to Point Imperial and other scenic lookout points. You can make a visit to Walhalla Glades Ruins along a self-guided trail. Make sure to take advantage of the dining opportunities at the Grand Canyon Lodge, and don't forget to watch the sunrise from Point Imperial.

If you have more time to spend at the Grand Canyon, and you feel up to the task, I would suggest several day-hikes along the Rims or into the Canyon (refer to pages 132–135), or an overnight trek or multi-day adventure into some of the Canyon's more remote areas, like the Village of Supai in the western Grand Canyon. Don't forget to make advance room reservations in Supai Village (refer to page 145 for more information).

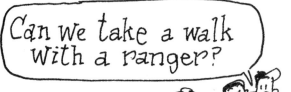

Can we take a walk with a ranger?

Let's go!

Year round on the South Rim, and from May 15–October 15 on the North Rim, you can join a ranger and get the inside scoop on the many facets of this amazing place. Many ranger-led programs include short hikes into the Canyon, as you learn about the history and geology around you. You can also join a ranger to help restore areas from invading plants, explore the fossil world inside the rock layers of the Canyon, watch a sunset, or discuss over a cup of coffee a subject that is of particular interest to you. Kids can also join "Junior Ranger" activities. To find out more about programs occuring during your visit, call the South Rim Visitor Center at (520) 638-7888 or the North Rim Visitor Center at (520) 638-7864. You can also check *The Guide* newspaper (South or North Rim editions) for times and locations.

Each evening, rangers give programs that explore the many aspects of the Grand Canyon. These progams include slide and video presentations. On the South Rim, evening programs are held from June to September in Mather Amphitheater, located behind the visitor center (be sure to dress warmly). From late September to mid-May, they're held in the Shrine of Ages building next to the visitor center. These programs are always entertaining and informative, and they're free.

At Desert View, rangers present programs on the Tusayan Ruins, an ancestral Pueblo village. From May to October, you can join a ranger for a fascinating guided walk through these ruins. During the fall (September–October), you can join a ranger and a representative of Hawkwatch International to identify raptors in flight over the Canyon. You can also join a ranger for a special sunset walk and viewing at beautiful Desert View Point. For more information, call the Desert View Information Center at (520) 638-7893.

On the North Rim, rangers offer daily talks and walks from Cape Royal. A special moonlight walk from the Grand Canyon Lodge to Bright Angel Point can be a moving experience. Evening campfire programs are presented in the campground ampitheater. Afternoon Lodge talks are also very entertaining.

NOTABLE GRAND CANYON ARCHITECTS

Charles Whittlesey: El Tovar Hotel (1905)

Francis Wilson: Santa Fe Grand Canyon Railroad Depot Building (1909)

Gilbert Underwood: Grand Canyon (North Rim) Lodge (1928)

Mary Elizabeth Jane Colter:
> Hopi House (1905)
> Lookout Studio (1914)
> Hermits Rest (1914)
> Phantom Ranch (1922)
> Desert View Watchtower (1932)
> Bright Angel Lodge (1935)
> Fred Harvey Men's Dormitory (1936)
> Colter Hall (1937)

Mary Colter at age 23 making a pottery bowl
Photo courtesy: Grand Canyon National Park
Museum Collection, #16952

Can we ride a mule into the Canyon?

Yes, you can still ride a mule to the Canyon floor. It's easier than hiking, and it gives you a chance to take your eyes off the trail and enjoy spectacular views during the descent.

Mule trips into the Grand Canyon have been offered since the 1880s, with the opening of the Bright Angel Trail. The saddle trips became so popular by the 1920s that Phantom Ranch was built in 1922 to accommodate the mule train guests. A distinction to remember is that you're on a mule—a cross between a horse and a donkey—not a donkey. Mules were bred as pack animals, with the ability to carry up to 200 pounds each, while the much smaller donkeys were bred for lighter domestic work.

South Rim. There are two types of mule trips you can make into the Canyon from the South Rim. One-day mule trips to Plateau Point depart daily year-round from the stone corral at the head of Bright Angel Trail. The ride descends about 3,200 feet to the Tonto Platform and Plateau Point, where you can see the Colorado River 1,320 feet below. This approximately seven-hour round trip departs at 8:00 a.m. during the summer and 9:00 a.m. during the winter. Cost is about $100 per person (prices subject to change). Other trips from the South Rim include an overnight to Phantom Ranch on Bright Angel Creek, where riders spend the night in ranch cabins and start the next day with a home-cooked breakfast (lunch and dinner also included). The first day's ride takes 5½ hours, followed by a 4½-hour trek on day two. Rides depart daily year-round from the stone corral at the head of Bright Angel Trail. Cost is about $524 per person for two people (the price goes down depending on the number of people in your party). Between November 15 and March 31 you can take a three-day, two-night trip to Phantom Ranch that gives you more time to relax and enjoy the scenery and ranch atmosphere. Prices are about $685 per person for parties of two, with prices varying depending upon the number of people.

For all of the popular South Rim mule trips, you'll need to make reservations well in advance. Call Amfac Parks & Resorts at (303) 29-PARKS, or write them at 14001 E. Iliff Avenue, Suite 600, Aurora, CO 80014. If you're in the park and do not have reservations, check at the Bright Angel Transportation Desk around 7:00 a.m. for cancellations. You can get information and purchase your mule trip at all Grand Canyon National Park Lodges transportation desks, including Bright Angel Lodge (6:00 a.m.–7:00 p.m. daily), Maswik Lodge (10:00 a.m.–4:00 p.m. daily), and Yavapai Lodge (9:00 a.m.–5:00 p.m., April–October). Information on mule trips is also available at the Fred Harvey desk at the visitor center (April–October, hours vary).

North Rim. On the less-visited North Rim, you can still ride a mule into the Canyon; you just have fewer choices. A bonus is that the rides cost less than on the South Rim. Half-day trips depart from the Grand Canyon Lodge daily during the season (May–October) at 7:30 a.m. and 12:30 p.m. On this trip, you'll descend 2,400 feet into the Canyon, to Supai Tunnel. A full-day trip also starts from the Lodge and descends 4,500 feet to Roaring Springs, where you'll enjoy lunch before your return. The cost for the half-day trip is $40 per person, and $95 per person for the full-

day trip. For reservations and information, call Canyon Trail Rides at (435) 679-8665.

All riders must weigh less than 200 pounds fully dressed, including equipment, be at least 4'7" in height, fluent in English, and not pregnant.

If you fit this description, get ready to saddle up and enjoy one of the most memorable rides anywhere.

Two women and a mule ascending Bright Angel Trail, 1910
Photo courtesy Grand Canyon National Park Museum Collection, #5433

Are there any self-guided tours of the Grand Canyon?

If you want to be your own guide, you have a variety of trails to choose from, in all areas of the park. This is a great way to view the sights and set your own pace. If you have questions after you've taken a self-guided tour, you can either join a ranger-led walk, or simply ask a ranger your questions by visiting a visitor center or information station on either Rim.

SOUTH RIM

There is a great self-guided walking tour of buildings that are designated landmarks in the historic district of Grand Canyon Village. On this easy 1.5-mile tour, you'll be able to visit nine historic buildings: 1) the Santa Fe Railway Station; 2) El Tovar Hotel; 3) Hopi House; 4) Verkamp's Curios; 5) Bright Angel Lodge; 6) Buckey O'Neill's Cabin; 7) Lookout Studio; 8) Kolb Studio; and 9) Red Horse Station. Depending on how long you want to stay at each building, this tour could take you one to two hours. A word of warning: some of the stairs between these buildings are steep, and you may require assistance.

You can also create your own self-guided tour by walking along the 9-mile Rim Trail, stopping at lookout points and interpretive signs along the way. Restrooms are available at Bright Angel Lodge and El Tovar Hotel.

Another interesting site on the South Rim that can be explored by self-guided tour is the Grand Canyon Cemetery, located just west of the Shrine of Ages building (see map, page 25). The cemetery has 304 plots reserved for people who have contributed greatly to the park, like early settlers, prospectors, trail guides, and government officials, as well as people who have worked in the park and their immediate families. As you walk among the headstones, you'll read names like John Hance, W. W. Bass, Pete Berry, Ralph Cameron, the Kolb brothers, John Verkamp, and Gunnar Widforss. There is even a memorial to the 128 passengers killed in the 1956 collision of United and TWA airliners that occurred 20,000 feet above the Canyon.

The Tusayan Museum and Ruins located along Desert View (East Rim) Drive (a 30-minute drive from Grand Canyon Village) provides visitors with a wonderful opportunity to explore the site of an 800-year-old ancestral *pueblo,* or village. After you walk through the settlement site, you can visit the museum, which displays many of the artifacts uncovered during the excavation of the site in the 1930s.

NORTH RIM

Along this rim you can take several easy self-guided walks. Here are some highlights:

⇨ Pick up a brochure from the Grand Canyon Lodge or the log shelter located in the parking lot of the lodge and enjoy a one-half mile (round trip) self-guided nature walk along the Bright Angel Point Trail.

⇨ The Widforss Trail starts from the parking lot just off the park entrance road, two miles north of Grand Canyon Lodge. The first 2.5 miles of this trail is an easy self-guided tour with brochures located at the trailhead.

⇨ There is a wonderful 0.8 mile self-guided loop tour of the Walhalla Glades Ruin, an ancestral Pueblo farming site located off the Cape Royal Road on the North Rim. From the walking tour brochure (found in a dispenser box at the site) you can explore 13 different sites, including living and farming areas that wind over alluvial terraces and drainages. Allow at least 45 minutes for the round trip tour.

⇨ The half-mile Cape Royal Trail begins at the southeast side of the Cape Royal parking lot. Take this self-guided trail a little more than a quarter of a mile, and you will arrive at Angels Window and the Cape Royal Overlook, with a spectacular view of the Colorado River.

what do you like best about the North Rim?

There aren't any people!

CAPE ROYAL OVERLOOK

How can we avoid the crowds?

There is one simple trick to avoiding the throngs of Grand Canyon visitors: don't come in the summer. However, if summer is your only vacation opportunity, the next best thing is to walk along the North Rim or South Rim, or down a Canyon trail—anywhere other than the teeming South Rim Village area. Since most of our visitors stay on the main South Rim Trail, you can lose the crowd by taking the less-frequented North Rim trails or the South Rim trails that descend into the Canyon. Some of the shorter South Rim trails (less than 10 miles) include South Kaibab Trail to Cedar Ridge (3 miles round trip) and Bright Angel Trail to Indian Garden (9 miles round trip). Some of our wilderness trails aren't as regularly maintained, and might require some route-finding skills due to washouts and large boulders. If you're up for this kind of experience, try Grandview Trail to Horseshoe Mesa (6 miles round trip, steep and narrow), or Hermit Trail to Santa Maria Springs (5 miles round trip, steep and narrow). On the North Rim, you can try the self-guiding Bright Angel Point Trail (½ mile round trip), Cape Royal Trail (½ mile round trip), Cliff Springs Trail (1 mile round trip), Transept Trail (3 miles round trip), the self-guiding Widforss Trail (5 miles round trip), Widforss Point (10 miles round trip), and the historic Uncle Jim Trail (10 miles round trip).

No matter where you hike, be sure to check at a visitor center for current trail conditions and closures. Things to bring along include a comfortable daypack, one gallon of water per person on hot days, snacks, layered clothing, walking or hiking shoes or boots, a hat and shirt to shield you from the sun, a first-aid kit, a flashlight (in case you don't get back to the rim before dark), and a map and compass. Lastly, but most importantly, make sure you pick a trail that matches your stamina, and won't aggravate any past injuries. For more information about hiking the Grand Canyon, refer to the "Recreational Opportunities" section of this book.

What are the best spots and best times to take pictures?

That's easy at a place like the Grand Canyon, where the sun shines bright all day and almost every spot offers scenic vistas.

The best times to take photos are mornings and evenings, when the sun is low in the sky and shadows add dimension and atmosphere to your pictures. Try to avoid mid-day shots, when the normally brilliant colors of the Canyon appear to be washed out by the sun's rays. If you can, let clouds add drama to your photographs. Thunderstorms that hit the Canyon during July and August offer particularly good opportunities to capture the dramatic buildup of storm clouds, as well as the aftermath of rain-soaked canyon vistas.

It's a little harder to advise you on the best places to take your photos, but here are some quick suggestions. Try a sunrise shot at Yaki, Mather, Lipan, or Yavapai Points (refer to page 35 for sunrise times). For a shot of the Colorado River, try a telephoto lens from Desert View, Pima, Hopi, Mohave, Yavapai, Moran, and Lipan Points. You can take a chance on getting some shots under a full moon over the Canyon or a lightning storm at night, but you'll need a tripod or solid rest for an exposure of about one to ten seconds or more. Photos of animals at the Canyon are best taken in the early morning or evening, around the ponderosa pine forests near Grand Canyon Village and at the North Rim. Wildflowers and flowering cacti start blooming in the Canyon in early spring, especially in hanging gardens at seeps and around the river. North Rim wildflowers begin their season in April, and South Rim wildflowers begin their season in June. Finally, you can photograph many interesting rock formations in the Canyon; for a better picture, zoom in on the formation of your choice to isolate it.

As for the kind of film to use, I would advise ISO 200–400, which is available at most of the gift stores and galleries throughout the park. For more tips on equipment, a Kodak representative leads photo walks from the front porch of El Tovar and other locations during July and August. For times, check *The Guide* newspaper or call the South Rim Visitor Center at (520) 638-7888. During the rest of the year, you can get advice directly from Kodak by calling (800) 242-2424.

How do the seasons affect getting around in the park?

The really big change around here happens in the winter, when the park becomes much less crowded and opens its arms to the many animals that are year-round residents.

South Rim. The roads all around the South Rim can be icy or covered in snow, so driving around the park becomes more hazardous. At night, it's not unusual to experience freezing temperatures that will make you wish you had brought your long johns to the Grand Canyon. Winter is quite a wonderful time around here, as the crowds have thinned out, the daytime weather is fairly moderate, and there is a special majesty to the Canyon when viewed under late afternoon light. Most of the South Rim visitor services are open for business, while a few close up shop until summer.

Inner Canyon. During the winter months, the temperature in the Canyon is at its best, with no intense heat during the day, and only an occasional freeze during the night. Winter is a time when you're more likely to see Canyon animals enjoying their habitat, without the scorching daytime summer temperatures.

North Rim. During the winter, the road to the North Rim closes, and most of this part of the park is closed to visitors. There are a few winter guests who snowshoe or cross-country ski into the North Rim, and then hike across the Canyon, but they're rare. The North Rim in the winter is even more remote and quiet than it is during the rest of the year. Although there are no services within park boundaries, visitors can still find gas, food, and lodging in Jacob Lake and Fredonia, Arizona, as well as Kanab and St. George, Utah.

IV

Lodging and Dining

Where... can ...we... stay... in ... the ... park ?

After a day of walking a rim trail or riding a mule to Plateau Point, a shower and a comfortable bed can be a great way to end the day. From May 15 to October 15, you have quite a few lodgings to choose from. There are nearly 1,480 overnight accommodations in nine lodgings (eight inside the park, and one at the park's south entrance).

Year-round, you can pick from almost as many accommodations on the South Rim and at Phantom Ranch in the Canyon. Rooms range from rustic cabins without baths to a suite in the El Tovar Hotel. For advance reservations at any of the Grand Canyon National Park Lodges, call Amfac Parks & Resorts at (303) 29-PARKS, fax a request to (303) 297-3175, or visit their website at www.amfac.com. If you're in the park and you want to check on cancellations to make same-night reservations, call (520) 638-2631. Remember, if you want your first choice, make your reservations up to 23 months in advance, especially for the summer season. (All rates subject to change.)

SOUTH RIM

Built by the Fred Harvey Company in 1905, the **El Tovar Hotel** is the architectural crown jewel of the Grand Canyon, a work of art along the Rim designed to complement the pinyon pine landscape that surrounds it as well as the natural beauty of the Canyon. The hotel is a National Historic Landmark, and is the Grand Canyon's most luxurious lodging. Refurbished in 1997, it boasts Oregon pine and native stone interiors that recall the old hunting lodges of Europe; it is the first example of rustic architecture in a national park. Today it has 127 rooms, ranging from suites for $279 to standard rooms with a double bed for $114. For information about ongoing art exhibits and activities in the hotel, or to check on same-night reservations, call (520) 638-2631. No pets.

Located just west of the El Tovar, the **Thunderbird and Kachina Lodges** were built in the 1960s to provide contemporary accommodations. The two-story identical structures are within easy walking distance of the Canyon rim and Grand Canyon Village. Registration for the Thunderbird Lodge is at the Bright Angel Lodge, and registration for the Kachina Lodge is at the El Tovar Hotel. The Thunderbird and Kachina Lodges offer well-appointed rooms with Canyon or park views. Prices range from $110 for a park-view room to $120 for a Canyon-view room. Contact the Bright Angel Lodge or El Tovar Hotel for more information. No pets.

Built from the remains of historic Bright Angel Camp in 1935, the **Bright Angel Lodge** offers a choice of lodge rooms and rustic cabins along the Canyon rim. Designed by architect Mary Colter, this log and native-stone structure has been called her crowning Grand Canyon achievement, with its environmentally-sensitive, pioneer-style design and construction. A large wooden thunderbird which she called "the Bright Angel of the sky" hangs above the mantle of the lobby's huge stone fireplace. Prices range from $45 for a basic room in the hiker's lodge to $117 for one of the special rim cabins (some have fireplaces). For about $230 you can stay in "Buckey's Cabin," which has a fireplace, two TVs, a sitting room, and a bar. No pets.

For budget-minded visitors, the **Maswik Lodge**, located at the southwest end of Grand Canyon Village, offers 278 modern lodge rooms and cabins each with shower and telephone. Named for the Hopi *kachina* (spirit) who guards the Grand Canyon, the lodge is open year-round, with the cabins available from May to October. Prices range from about $60 for a cabin, to $114 for a room in the north wing of the lodge. No pets.

Nestled among the pinyon and juniper pygmy forests between Yavapai Point and the El Tovar Hotel is the park's largest lodging facility, **Yavapai Lodge**. It features year-round, modern motel-style accommodations in its east and west wings, while the main lodge provides registration, dining, and gift stores. The 358 units range in price from $85 in Yavapai West, to $100 in Yavapai East. No pets.

Located in the Kaibab National Forest just outside the park's south entrance, **Moqui Lodge** features rustic ponderosa pine interiors and 136 rooms that include full baths, showers, ceiling fans, and color TVs. There's also a riding stable, Mexican restaurant, cocktail lounge, Mobil service station, and gift shop. Open April to October. No pets.

INNER CANYON

Nestled beside Bright Angel Creek and a stand of cottonwood trees on the floor of the Inner Canyon, you'll find the Western-style cabins and main lodge of **Phantom Ranch**—an oasis that recalls the ranch hospitality of another era. Built in 1922, the Ranch's 82 beds are the only accommodation in the Canyon, and can only be reached by hiking, by mule, or by rafting the Colorado River. Prices vary depending on your mode of transportation. If you hike down, you can reserve a cabin with four to ten bunkbeds for about $66, or a bed in one of the newer dorm buildings for about $24. Hearty meals will run you about $29 for a steak dinner, $18 for the hiker's stew, $8 for lunch, and $13 for breakfast. If you arrive on a mule, you'll pay about $295 per person for one night (includes all meals and cabin accommodations) or $524 for two people (all rates subject to change). If you want to make it a two-night stay, you're looking at $409 per person or $685 for two people. Because summer temperatures can reach 110 degrees Fahrenheit on the Canyon floor, the best time to visit Phantom Ranch is from November to March. But beware, the secret's out about Phantom. You'll have to book a place here well in advance (up to 23 months) to get a chance to experience the Ranch and its unique wilderness setting.

NORTH RIM

Designed by Gilbert Stanley Underwood (legendary architect of the Ahwahnee Hotel in Yosemite), the **Grand Canyon Lodge** opened its doors to its first visitors in 1928. Designed as one of the great national park lodges, it's a National Historic Landmark featuring ponderosa pine and native stone throughout the main building. From the veranda and lounge areas, you can enjoy spectacular views of the Canyon through enormous plate glass windows and expansive terraces. Its 167 cabins and 40 motel units are scattered near the main lodge building, in the ponderosa forest. Prices vary depending upon the type of guest accommodations. Motel units go for $81, and there are three types of cabins, ranging from $75 for the smallest Frontier Cabin to $95 for a large Western Cabin near the rim.

If you bring your own room in the form of a recreational vehicle, you can reserve space at Trailer Village year-round. There are 84 sites with full hook-ups for hard-sided vehicles only. Showers and laundry facilities are available nearby. Cost per space is $20 with a seven-day limit. Call Amfac Parks & Resorts at (303) 29-PARKS to reserve a space at least six months in advance. Or, you can try (520) 638-2631 for same-day reservations.

If you're in the park and you haven't made reservations, you can always take a chance and check with any of the lodging desks about last-minute cancellations, or call (520) 638-2631. Although visitors do cancel their reservations from time to time, this is not a recommended way to find a place to stay in the park, especially during our summer season.

Are there convenient places to stay just outside the park?

You can find lodging in several places near Grand Canyon National Park. Here are some options near the South and North Rims.

SOUTH RIM

Tusayan (2 miles south of entrance). This collection of lodgings is closest to the park entrance. For detailed information and pictures of these accommodations, check out www.thecanyon.com.

Best Western Grand Canyon Squire Inn Highway 64 (800) 622-6966	$65–$225, seasonal rates 250 rooms, 4 suites

Southwestern decor resort hotel with Coronado Room Restaurant, coffee shop, pool, billiards, bowling, and video arcade.

Quality Inn and Suites Grand Canyon Highway 64 (520) 638-2673 (800) 221-2222	$73–$188, seasonal rates 176 rooms, 56 suites

A full service resort with buffet and restaurant, lounge, gift shop, seasonal outdoor pool and indoor spa. All rooms with private balconies or patios.

Grand Hotel Highway 64 (520) 638-3333 (888) 63-GRAND	$79–$138, seasonal rates 120 rooms

Grand Canyon's newest hotel with distinctive Southwestern decor, heated indoor pool and Canyon Star Restaurant.

Holiday Inn Express Hotel and Suites Highway 64 (520)638-3000 (800) HOLIDAY	$69–$250, seasonal rates (includes breakfast) 197 rooms, 32 suites

Award-winning Holiday Inn has merged with the Grand Canyon Suites to offer, in addition to their Holiday rooms, stylish "Arizona Rooms" of one- and two-bedroom suites reminiscent of historic park lodges.

Rodeway Inn: Red Feather Lodge Highway 64 (520) 638-2414	$56–$119, seasonal rates 231 rooms

(800) 228-2000
Canyon visitors with small pets welcome here! Heated pool, video game room, and Cafe Tusayan restaurant.

(Seven Mile Lodge is also located in Tusayan, but it does not take reservations. You'll get a room at this small, affordable lodge on a first-come, first-served basis. Call them for more information at (520) 638–2291.)

Valle (27 miles from the south entrance) Valle offers various visitor services including two gas stations, an amusement park and campground, and a small airport with air museum.

Grand Canyon Lodge $49-$89, seasonal
Junction of Highways 180 & 64   101 rooms
Valle, Arizona
Mailing: PO Box 702, Williams, AZ 86046
(520) 635-9203
Seasonal pool, full service restaurant, and gift shop.

Williams, "Gateway to the Grand Canyon." Williams is located in the heart of the beautiful Kaibab National Forest. It is 60 miles from the south entrance of the park, at an elevation of 6,770 feet. You can stay closer to the park, in Tusayan or Grand Canyon Village, but the closer you get, the more you will pay. Check out www.thegrandcanyon.com for more details about lodging and special events in this historic Southwestern town.

Canyon Country Inn B & B $55–$120, seasonal rates
442 W. Route 66   (includes breakfast)
(520) 635-2349   13 rooms
Charming teddy bear theme with delicious "beary" specials in the morning. Private baths.

New Canyon Motel $30–$60, seasonal rates
1900 E. Rodeo Rd.   18 rooms in 6 cabins
(520) 635-9371
(800) 482-3955
Set in a lush pine forest. Heated indoor pool. Charming rooms all have TVs; some have kitchenettes.

Mountain Country Lodge B & B $50–$100 year-round
437 W. Route 66   (includes breakfast)
(520) 635-4341   9 rooms
(800) 973-6210
Historic 1909 mansion. Each charming room has a private bath. Hearty continental breakfast to start your day.

Mountain Side Inn $66–$86, seasonal rates
642 E. Bill Williams Ave.   96 rooms
(520) 635-4431
(800) 462-9381
High country comforts overlooking 27 pine-filled acres. Heated pool and
choice of hearty fare in Miss Kitty's Steakhouse and Saloon or the casual
Dining Car Restaurant.

The Red Garter Bed & Bakery $65–$105, seasonal rates
137 W. Railroad Ave.   4 rooms
(520) 635-1484
(800) 328-1484
Rave reviews from guests of this beautifully restored Victorian bordello and
saloon. Listed in National Register of Historic Places. Comfortable rooms
with names like "Best Gal's Room" and "Madam's Room," plus great
breakfasts.

Sheridan House Inn $110–$225
460 E. Sheridan   (includes breakfast)
(520) 635-9441   8 rooms
(888) 635-9345
Country charm in this art-filled house on 2 acres of pine forest. Evening
social hour, bountiful breakfast buffet, outdoor spa. Lovely decks and a
flagstone patio surround this distinctive inn.

Terry Ranch B & B $100–$140, seasonal rates
701 Quarterhorse Rd.   (includes breakfast)
(520) 635-4171   4 rooms
(800) 210-5908
Spacious rooms in country Victorian decor, located at the foot of Bill
Williams Mountain. Two rooms have fireplaces.

Grand Canyon KOA
(closes during winters) $18.50–$40
N. Arizona Highway 64
(520) 635-2307
(800) KOA-5771
For those on wheels, this quiet off-highway campground offers indoor
pool, convenience facilities and 12 "Kamping Kabins" for rent.
Reservations needed June–August.

Flagstaff (89 miles from park entrance). Although a bit further from the park, you can find nice lodging in these facilities.

Arizona Mountain Inn B & B
4200 Lake Mary Rd.
(520) 774-8959
(800) 239-5236

$80–$390, seasonal rates
(includes breakfast)
3 rooms, 16 cottages

Beautiful old English inn in the pines. The cottages have kitchens and fireplaces. There is also one apartment for rent, nightly or by the month.

Best Western Pony Soldier
3030 E. Route 66
(800) 356-4143

$59–$99, seasonal rates
(includes continental
breakfast) (520) 526-2388
90 rooms

A life-size pony marks this two-story motel decorated in Southwestern motif. Heated indoor pool. Jalapeño Lou's Restaurant on premises.

Birch Tree Inn B & B
824 W. Birch Ave.
(520) 774-1042
(888) 774-1042

$55–$119, seasonal rates
(includes breakfast and
afternoon snacks)
5 rooms

Traditional B&B one-half mile from downtown. Three rooms with private bath, fireplace, hot tub, pool table.

Hilton Garden Inn
350 W. Forest Meadow St.
(520) 226-8888
(800) 333-0785

$69–$129, seasonal rates
90 rooms

Heated indoor pool and exercise room. All rooms have TV and fridges. Next door to Coco's Bakery Restaurant.

InnSuites Hotel
1008 E. Route 66
(520) 774-7356
(800) 898-9124

$49–$139, seasonal rates
(includes breakfast buffet)
130 rooms, 15 suites

Complimentary evening beverage service and Wednesday BBQ for guests, all in a lovely pine forest setting.

Little America Hotel
2515 E. Butler Ave.
(520) 779-2741
(800) 865-1399

$65–$119, seasonal rates
246 rooms

Luxurious rooms on 500 acres of ponderosa forest. Heated pool, dining room (great brunch on Sundays!), coffee shop, TV.

Radisson Woodlands Hotel $69–$129
1175 W. Route 66 183 rooms, 17 suites
(520) 773-8888
(800) 333-3333
Elegance and comfort with heated pool and hot tub. Southwestern flavors
in the Woodlands Cafe, or entertaining Japanese teppan-style cooking in
Sakura Restaurant and Sushi Bar.

NORTH RIM

Kaibab Lodge (5 miles north of park entrance)
Highway 67 $75–$125
(520) 638-2389 (May–October only)
(520) 526-0924 (November–May)
This lodge is open during the season only, from May through October. It
includes a restaurant and campground.

Jacob Lake (32 miles north of park entrance)

Jacob Lake Inn $69–$109, seasonal rates
Intersection of Highways 89A & 67 40 rooms
(520) 643-7232

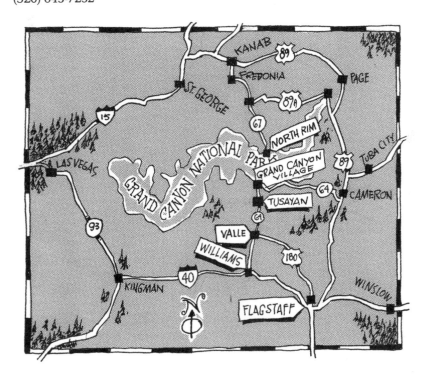

Where can we eat in the park?

Grand Canyon offers a full range of dining and snacking experiences, from historic dining rooms to casual cafeterias, fast-food joints, delis, and fountain shops. Kids get their own menus, the dress is always casual, and all eating areas are non-smoking. Prices range from around $4 for breakfast at the Bright Angel Coffee Shop to almost $30 for a complete meal at the El Tovar Hotel. Many of the restaurants accept American Express, VISA, MasterCard, and Diners Club. If you want to make reservations or need more information, call (520) 638-2631.

SOUTH RIM

The fanciest evening meals on the South Rim of the Grand Canyon are served in the dining room at the **El Tovar Hotel**. The menu includes such fare as prime rib, steak, seafood, chicken, vegetarian, and daily specials, with prices that won't break the bank. Full-service breakfast and lunch are also served. Advance reservations are advised, as guests without reservations often have a long wait. Another good choice is the **Arizona Steakhouse**, located next to the Bright Angel Lodge on the Rim. Here you'll enjoy dinner selections of wonderful broiled steaks, poultry, and seafood in a comfortable Western atmosphere. Open only for dinner, and closed January–February. The **Moqui Lodge Dining Room**, located just outside the south entrance to the park, serves up delicious and moderately priced Mexican and American entrees, with a vegetarian special nightly. Breakfast (until 10:00 a.m.) and dinner (from 6:00 p.m.) served daily, with no reservations accepted. Closed November–March.

Casual dining can be enjoyed at the **Bright Angel Lodge Dining Room and Coffee Shop**, where dinner entrees include a wide selection of hearty meals, including vegetarian. Breakfast (6:30 a.m.–10:45 a.m.), lunch (11:15 a.m.–10:00 p.m.), and dinner (4:00 p.m.–10:00 p.m.) served daily.

If quick and easy eating is your goal, try one of the park's three cafeterias located at **Desert View Trading Post** (year-round), **Maswik Lodge** (year-round), and **Yavapai Lodge** (March–December). Self-service entrees and a la carte selections include salads, sandwiches, pasta, chicken, and pizza. All three cafeterias are open for breakfast, lunch, and dinner.

Fast-food options are found throughout the park. For quick snacks at one of the South Rim's most popular gathering places, check out the **Fountain at the Bright Angel Lodge**. It offers hot dogs, sandwiches, ice cream, and cold drinks from May through September. Prices are reasonable, and it's open from 8:00 a.m. to 4:00 p.m. daily. Or, try the deli at the **Delaware North Park Services** store (formerly Babbitt's General Store) located across from the visitor center. There you can get hot and cold sandwiches, chicken dinners, salads, and daily specials to eat there or to go. **Hermits Rest Snack Bar,** located next to Hermits Rest Gift Shop at the end of Hermit Road, offers quick snacks including hot dogs and light fare to go. Lounges offering drinks and light snacks are located in most lodging facilities, including Bright Angel Lodge, Maswik Lodge, Moqui Lodge, and the El Tovar Hotel.

For a dining experience that is pure Grand Canyon, don't forget the twilight campfire trail and wagon ride that leaves Moqui Lodge nightly from May until the first snow. You'll board an old-fashioned wagon or ride horseback from Moqui Lodge to an Old West campfire in Kaibab National Forest, where you'll cook your own food over the campfire. The cost is $40 per person for the trail ride and $12.50 for riding in the wagon. For more information, call Apache Stables at (520) 638-2891, or inquire at any lodging activity desk. This is a popular activity and tends to book up fast, especially the trail ride.

INNER CANYON
If you're lucky enough to get a reservation at **Phantom Ranch,** you'll be treated to some great homestyle dining at the Canteen. A bountiful, family-style menu includes a hiker's stew, steak dinner, country breakfast, and sack lunch. You'll need to reserve in advance, with all meals served at prearranged times.

NORTH RIM
From April to October you have several dining options on the North Rim, with prices to suit every budget. The fanciest meals can be enjoyed in the **Grand Canyon Lodge Dining Room,** which serves continental meals with spectacular views of the Canyon. Breakfast (6:30 a.m.–10:00 a.m.), lunch (11:30 a.m.–2:30 p.m.), and dinner (5:00 p.m.–9:30 p.m.) are served daily, with dinner reservations required. You can pick up quick snacks at inexpensive prices at the **Lodge Snack Shop,** open daily during the season from 6:30 a.m.–9:00 p.m. The Lodge also offers visitors the **North Rim Saloon and Coffee Bar,** offering light snacks at great prices daily from 11:00 a.m.–10:30 p.m. The **General Store,** located across from the North Rim campground, has pizzas, snacks, and groceries at reasonable prices. It's open daily from 8:00 a.m.–8:00 p.m. (hours can vary with demand).

There are many good places to eat near Grand Canyon National Park. Here are just a few of them.

South Rim

TUSAYAN (2 MILES SOUTH OF PARK ENTRANCE):

You can find the usual assortment of fast-food places here plus restaurants in most of the hotels. If you have more time, you might want to try these establishments.

Canyon Star
Grand Hotel
Highway 64
(520) 638-3553
Delicious steaks, BBQ, live entertainment, western music, canyon-lands video. Breakfast, lunch, dinner, cocktails.

Grand Canyon Quality Inn and Suites
Highway 64
(520) 638-2673
The restaurant at this Quality Inn serves Southwestern and American home-cooked specialties, at your table or buffet style. Breakfast, lunch, dinner, cocktails.

WILLIAMS (60 MILES FROM THE SOUTH ENTRANCE TO THE PARK):

Here are a few food joints to check out in Williams.

Cruiser's Cafe 66
233 W. Route 66
(520) 635-2445
This shrine to the "Mother Road" is great for families. It features an old gas station setting, along with foods such as calzones, steaks, ribs, and chicken. Lunch, dinner, cocktails.

Grand Canyon Coffee & Cafe
125 W. Route 66
(520) 635-1255
Grab your favorite coffee steamer or espresso, hot or frosted, plus bagels, sandwiches, salads. Breakfast, lunch, dinner.

Miss Kitty's Steakhouse & Saloon
642 E. Route 66
(520) 635-9161
Steaks, prime rib, BBQ chicken, plus live music on stage in the summer. Breakfast and dinner, cocktails.

Pancho McGillicuddy's
141 Railroad Ave.
(520) 635-4150
Williams's first Old West saloon sets the theme for fun at this Mexican cantina. Lunch, dinner, cocktails.

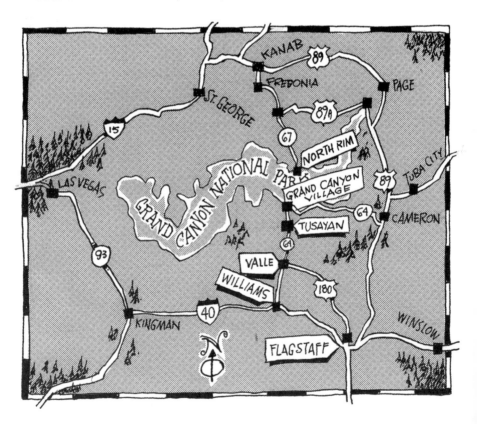

Pine Country Restaurant
107 N. Grand Canyon Blvd.
(520) 635-9718
Good home cooking, homemade pies a specialty. Breakfast, lunch, dinner. No adult beverages.

Rod's Steakhouse
301 E. Route 66
(520) 635-2671
Any restaurant in the same location for more than 50 years is doing something right! The name says it all—go for the beef. Lunch, dinner, cocktails.

Rosa's Cantina
106 S. 9th St.
(520) 635-0708
All spicy things Mexican, and great margaritas in the Double Deuce Cantina. Lunch, dinner, cocktails.

FLAGSTAFF (80 MILES FROM THE SOUTH ENTRANCE):
All restaurants below are open 7 days a week, hours vary. Major credit cards accepted.

Beaver Street Brewery & Whistlestop Cafe
11 S. Beaver St.
(520) 779-0079
Wood-fired pizzas, specialty sandwiches, soup, salads, fondue. Lunch, dinner, cocktails.

Black Bart's Steakhouse
& Musical Revue
2760 E. Butler Ave.
(520) 779-3142
Nightly musical revue with your steak, chicken, seafood, or ribs. Dinner, cocktails.

Bun Hugger East
3012 E. Route 66
(520) 526-0542

Bun Hugger West
901 S. Milton Rd.
(520) 779-3743

Best mesquite-grilled burgers and sandwiches around. Lunch, dinner, cocktails.

Chez Marc
503 N. Humphreys St.
(520) 774-1343
Country French dining in historic house. Lunch, dinner, cocktails.

Cottage Place Restaurant
126 W. Cottage Ave.
(520) 774-8431
Fine dining in restored 1909 bungalow. Dinner. Closed Mondays. Beer & wine only.

Mama Luisa
2710 N. Steves Blvd.
(520) 526-6809
Delicious Italian fare in casual, cozy setting. Dinner, cocktails.

Mason Jar Restaurant
2610 E. Route 66
(520) 526-1399
Cobblers and home-style cookin'—as American as Route 66. Breakfast, lunch, dinner, cocktails.

North Rim

Kaibab Lodge Dining Room (5 miles north of park entrance)
Jacob Lake Road
(520) 638-2389
Serves good and hearty breakfast, lunch, and dinners from May 15–October 15 only.

Jacob Lake Inn Coffee Shop & Dining Room (32 miles north of park entrance)
Intersection of Highways 89A & 67
(520) 643-7232
Serves up a hearty breakfast, lunch, and dinner year-round. Home-cooked American fare with local specialities including baked trout and fresh baked goods. Reasonable prices—an entire meal will run you $5.95.

Where can we pick up picnic supplies?

With nearly 25 established picnic areas situated near some of the park's most scenic lookouts on both the South and North Rims, Grand Canyon is the ultimate picnic spot. Where you finally decide to spread your tablecloth is up to you, but here are some choices for stocking up on goods.

If you don't want to do the legwork, you can pick up a box lunch from the cafeteria at Maswik Lodge, open 6:00 a.m. to 10:00 p.m. Box lunches cost $7.60 and include a choice of sandwich, a piece of fruit, a drink, peanuts, chips, and a cookie.

For sandwiches and drinks made to order and to go, you have lots of options, including the delicatessens at the three Delaware North Park Services stores (formerly Babbitt's General Stores). These stores, which will be renamed in 2000, are located near the visitor center in Grand Canyon Village, at Desert View, and in Tusayan. Or, if you want to put together your own picnic supplies, cruise the grocery aisles of these stores.

Are there any special seasonal events in the Grand Canyon?

You bet. During the first three weeks of September, the park hosts the Grand Canyon Music Festival at the Shrine of Ages auditorium, next to the visitor center on the South Rim. Cosponsored by the National Park Service, the festival brings musicians from across the country to perform concerts to sold-out audiences of residents and visitors alike. Tickets cost about $18 and can be purchased in advance by calling the Grand Canyon Music Festival at (800) 997-8285 or (520) 638-9215. You can also purchase tickets at the door, unless the performance is sold out. You can write to the music festival at P.O. Box 1332, Grand Canyon, Arizona 86023 or visit them online at www.grandcanyonmusicfest.org.

Throughout the year, the El Tovar Hotel hosts events including art exhibits, Native American craft markets, and music performances for the enjoyment of park visitors. Call (520) 638-2631 for more information and a schedule of activities.

During the winter, Grand Canyon celebrates the holidays with Christmas festivities and cheer, including a 20-foot-tall Christmas tree in the lobby of the El Tovar, and a Christmas Eve and Christmas night celebration at Phantom Ranch, hosted by the ranch hands. For more information on events around the Colorado Plateau Area, including Flagstaff and Williams, refer to the telephone numbers listed on page 208 in "Quick Reference."

V

Camping and Backpacking

Be careful. It's a jungle out there.

It wouldn't be one of our great national parks without a slew of camping choices. Let's run down the options in each area, from pitching a tent to hooking up your fully equipped RV. Of course, camping prices are subject to change.

South Rim

Camping on the South Rim is generally restricted to established campgrounds, although a few remote sites are available with a backcountry permit. Coin-operated laundry and showers are available near Mather Campground, and stay open from 7:00 a.m. to 9:00 p.m. A sanitary dump station is located near Mather and Trailer Village, and is open from mid-May through mid-October.

Mather Campground

Mather, located near the visitor center in Grand Canyon Village, is a large campground run by the National Park Service (NPS). There are 326 individual tent and RV sites (no hookups available), and reservations are strongly recommended from March 1 to December 1. Reservations can be made up to five months in advance, with sites costing $12 to $15. The rest of the year, Mather operates on a first-come, first-served basis, at a price of about $10 per site. For reservations, call (800) 638-2267 (water and restrooms, group sites available).

Trailer Village

Trailer Village, open year-round, is adjacent to Mather campground. It offers RV sites with hookups at a cost of about $20 per site for two people, and around $1.75 for each additional person. Reservations are recommended and can be made by calling (303) 297-2757. Campers can register at the entrance to Trailer Village (water, electric, sewer available).

Desert View Campground Desert View Campground, open mid-May through mid-October, is located near the east entrance, 25 miles east of Grand Canyon Village. There are no hookups and no reservations, just first-come, first-served at a cost of about $10 per site (water and toilets available).

Inner Canyon There are only three developed campgrounds in the Inner Canyon, all of which are located along the corridor trails. They are: **Indian Garden Campground** below the South Rim; **Bright Angel Campground** near Phantom Ranch; and **Cottonwood Campground** below the North Rim. All three require backcountry permits. All other camping permits for the Inner Canyon are issued for sites without water, toilets, emergency phones, or similar amenities (for more details on backcountry camping, see pages 117–121).

North Rim

Camping on the North Rim is only possible from May 15 to October 16, weather permitting. Before or after these times, you're dealing with some serious weather. Come to think of it, you might get some nasty weather even when it's open. It's generally a rougher experience, with fewer facilities and visitor services.

North Rim Campground North Rim Campground is NPS-operated and located a mile from the Rim. There are 84 individual tent and RV sites (no hookups) at a price of about $15 to $20 per site. Reservations are strongly recommended and can be made by calling (800) 365-2267 (up to five months in advance). Coin-operated showers are located nearby, open 7:00 a.m. to 9:00 p.m. (water, restrooms, and group sites also available).

What are the campgrounds outside the park?

If you can't get a spot at one of the campgrounds inside the park, you can always try your luck at one of the sites outside park boundaries. We'll list your options according to area.

South Rim

The U.S. Forest Service operates a public campground (no hookups) at **Ten-X Campground**, located three miles south of Tusayan. It's open from May 1 to September 30. Try to get there early, as its 70 sites tend to fill up fast. Cost is around $10 per site, with picnic tables, fire rings, barbecue grills, water, and toilets. No showers or reservations. For more information, call (520) 638-2443 (group sites available).

You may also find a good place to camp in the national forest outside the park. Restrictions may apply; for example, camping is not allowed within a quarter-mile of Highway 64. For more information, call (520) 638-2443, or write the Tusayan Ranger District, Kaibab National Forest, P.O. Box 3088, Grand Canyon, AZ 86023.

You RV cowboys may find a place to park at **Camper Village**, a privately run operation open year-round in Tusayan. Fees range from about $15 per day for a tent to $23 for trailer space with water, electric, and sewer. There's also a general store, food service, and miniature golf. Call (520) 638-2887 for information.

North Rim

Like everything at the North Rim, camping outside the park here is seasonal, and depends greatly on the weather. **DeMotte Campground**, run by the U.S. Forest Service, is located five miles north of the park entrance station. It's open May to October, available on a first-come, first-served basis only, and offers water, pit toilets, grills, and picnic tables for about $10 a night (no hookups). Call (520) 643-7395 for more information.

Jacob Lake Campground, also located on national forest property, is 32 miles north of the entrance station. There are 50 sites available on a first-come, first-served basis during summers only. Cost is around $10 per car (no hookups). Call (520) 643-7395.

Kaibab Camper Village (open May 15–October 15 only) is privately run, and is located a quarter-mile south of Jacob Lake on Highway 67. Hookups are available, and you can make a reservation by calling (520) 643-7804 in the summer or (520) 526-0924 in the winter.

Dispersed camping is permitted in the national forest outside the park. This means no facilities, no water, and many regulations. To find out what they are, call the North Kaibab Ranger District at (520) 643-7395, or write their office at Kaibab National Forest, P.O. Box 248, Fredonia, AZ 86022.

Are there limits or restrictions on camping at Grand Canyon?

Y ou probably guessed the answer—yes, there are rules and restrictions. But it's all for a good cause, mainly to protect both you and the Canyon from unnecessary harm. Camping outside designated areas is prohibited and strictly monitored, and rule breakers may receive a hefty fine.

We hope our campers follow the golden rule of camping: Leave No Trace. That means packing out all your trash, keeping your fires in the grills, and not gathering wood. Wood and charcoal may be purchased at the general store. Remember, no open fires.

Squirrels, coyotes, and other campground scavengers are always on the prowl for goodies. Store food and any fragrant items (such as shampoo, toothpaste, and soap) safely out of reach, either in your car or in a backpack. You'll need to hang your backpacks from a tree or rack to keep the critters out.

Backcountry campers need to obtain a permit (see permit requirements, pages 177–178). They also need to follow a special set of rules to keep our wilderness areas as pristine as possible. Besides packing out trash and using campstoves instead of fires, you'll need to bury human waste at least 100 feet from trails, campsites, and water sources (bury waste at least six inches deep). Pack out toilet paper in plastic bags rather than burning or burying it. Many wildfires have been started by burning trash and toilet paper. Any washing (of clothes, bodies, dishes, etc.) should be done at least 100 feet from water sources.

Can we build a campfire?

A campfire's comforting crackle is one of the best parts of camping, but it has caused some of our forest fires. As long as you follow a few guidelines, our next generation of campers will be able to enjoy fireside gatherings as well.

Fires are prohibited below the Rims due to wood shortages and wildfire dangers. It's probably for the best; fire remains can be a real eyesore, and that charcoal and ash can take hundreds of years to break down in this arid climate. Also, collecting wood is not allowed anywhere in the park. Break that rule and you might collect a fine from a ranger. You can only build fires in the campgrounds where grills are provided. Ground fires and the building of fire rings are prohibited.

Now, some safety measures. Start by using those established fire pits, then check around the area for potential spark hazards. Never leave fires unattended; put them out by stirring in water before you leave the campground, and do a final check for any remaining embers. For the sake of protecting our wilderness environment, backpackers are asked to use small portable stoves for cooking and boiling water.

What special activities can we find around the campgrounds?

Campers often want to learn more about this awesome place called the Grand Canyon. That's where the ranger programs come in. Take a look at *The Guide* or visit a visitor center to find out more about all the available activities. Here's a sampling of programs that have been offered in the past by the park staff (note that the programs are subject to cancellation due to rain, snow, or lightning and may not be offered year-round).

One way to take in the wonder of the place while learning more about it is to join a ranger-led hike. The strenuous Kaibab Hike takes about two and a half hours, and goes one mile down a steep, unpaved trail to the appropriately named Ooh-Aah Point. The one-hour, leisurely Geology Walk explores the geologic events that created the Grand Canyon. The easy, one-mile Fossil Walk (one hour) takes you back 250 million years, to a time when sea creatures lived in the area. Come watch the ever-changing colors of "The Spirit Of Sunset," a half-mile stroll to scenic Canyon vistas. Dress warmly.

If you want to just kick back and take it all in, you can join a ranger for "Coffee On The Rim," a 30-minute get-together on the back porch of the El Tovar Hotel. The "Grand Canyon Grab Bag" is an hour-long question and answer session that meets at the Yavapai Observation Station.

There's also an opportunity to make a lasting impression on the Canyon by helping a Habitat Restoration Team battle non-native plants. It's called "Alien Invaders," a two-hour work party that meets in front of the visitor center.

Evening programs allow you to see the starlit side of the Canyon. Nightly activities meet at the Mather Amphitheater, located behind the visitor center (during the winter, they meet inside the Shrine of Ages next to the center). Allow an hour for the slideshow, dress warmly, and bring a flashlight.

In the Desert View area, there are a few programs designed to enhance your knowledge of the Canyon's history and wildlife. "Glimpses of the Past," which meets at the Tusayan Museum, focuses on the ancient people who called the Canyon home. Bring a book and binoculars to "Raptures in Flight" and "Hawk Migration." These two programs begin at the Lipan Point parking lot, three miles west of Desert View on East Rim Drive.

Where can we rent camping gear and buy supplies inside the park?

No matter how prepared you think you are for a camping excursion in the Grand Canyon, there's a chance some vital piece of equipment slipped through the cracks ("Honey, you forgot the tent and sleeping bags").

If you find yourself in the park, ready to camp but completely unprepared, head to one of the three Delaware North Park Services stores (formerly Babbitt's General Stores). These stores (which will be renamed in the year 2000), offer both sales and rentals of camping equipment. You can buy or rent tents, sleeping bags, sleeping pads, stoves, and fuel. They also have groceries, film, and other basic items. You can reach them at (520) 638-2262. The nearest place outside the park to find the full range of items is probably Flagstaff, Arizona, about 1.5–2 hours away.

Wherever you get your camping gear, make sure you have a tent with rainfly, ground cloth, warm sleeping bag, sleeping pad, flashlight, extra socks, food, cooking stove and fuel, pot, spoon, cup, water bottle, and any personal gear.

> ## Are there any organized trips into the backcountry?

There are so many, it will make your head spin. We're no longer dealing with simple options like, "Should I ride a mule, or walk?" Today you have a multitude of choices; in fact, there so many that I can't mention them all here. What I can do is to give you a sampling of some interesting stuff the backcountry outfitters are up to these days, then refer you to pages 187–190 for names and numbers.

The Grand Canyon Field Institute (GCFI) is the field seminar program for the Grand Canyon Association, cosponsored by the National Park Service. Classes explore the natural and cultural history of the Grand Canyon with dayhikes, backpacking, river trips, van camping, and more. During the spring and summer, you can take three-day introductory backpacking trips on the North Rim, South Rim, or Inner Canyon for about $200. In October the GCFI offers five-day geology exploration trips from Rim to Rim for about $300. There are natural history hikes, photography excursions, hikes just for women, llama treks, and many other options. For a complete listing of GCFI trips, call (520) 638-2485, write them at P.O. Box 399, Grand Canyon, AZ 86023, or visit their website at www.grandcanyon.org/fieldinstitute.

And that's just one of the organizations that offers trips! Around the Grand Canyon, you have lots of other adventure providers just waiting to dazzle the spirit with mountain bike trips, river excursions, horseback trips, and much more.

When and why do we need a backcountry permit?

A pessimist might say that backcountry permits (which cost $10 plus $5 per person, per night, but subject to change) are just another way for the NPS to make a profit. But permits serve a very important function: they allow rangers to protect both you and the park from overuse. Also, about 400 hikers (mostly dayhikers) per year need rescue assistance in the Grand Canyon. Believe me, those rescued hikers would be happy to pay for another permit.

A backcountry permit is required for all overnight use of the backcountry, including hiking, horseback-riding, cross-country ski trips, off-river hikes by river-trip members, and camping at rim sites other than developed campgrounds. Permits for all overnight use must be obtained through the Backcountry Information Center. And, once your itinerary is established, you are required to follow the exact plan authorized on the permit.

Every year, the demand for permits far outweighs the allowed use limits, which were established to protect the canyon and the quality of visitors' experience. For this reason, advance reservations are strongly recommended, and they can be made up to four months in advance. While the permit allows you access to the backcountry, it does not reserve a specific tent site within the backcountry.

THERE ARE FOUR WAYS TO APPLY FOR A PERMIT:

⇨ bring your request in person to the Backcountry Information Center;

⇨ make your request on the Internet (www.thecanyon.com/nps);

⇨ fax your request to the Backcountry Information Center at (520) 638-2125;

⇨ mail your request to the Backcountry Information Center, Grand Canyon National Park, P.O. Box 129, Grand Canyon, AZ 86023-0129. A request form and a summary of permit requirements can be found on pages 176–178.

For more information, call the Backcountry Information Center at (520) 638-7875 between 1:00 p.m. and 5:00 p.m (Mountain Standard Time), Monday through Friday, except federal holidays.

When is the best time of year to visit the Grand Canyon's backcountry?

I'd like to say anytime is the right time, but the Grand Canyon is a land of extremes, from the banks of the Colorado River to the high desert. My favorite time is in October—fewer crowds on the Rim, but among the busiest backcountry-use months, with normally moderate temperatures. Summer is very hot and very crowded, but sometimes that's the only time people can get away. Winter can be downright nasty, with icy and snowy conditions. The best time of year to explore the backcountry depends on what you want and are able to do. But all things being equal, your safest bets are the late spring and early fall. Here are some special considerations for those of you thinking about other times of the year.

South Rim. The South Rim is located on an exposed high desert with wildly fluctuating temperatures. When exploring the backcountry here in the summer, remember to be prepared for intense sun and drenching thunderstorms. Winter temperatures average about 30 degrees Fahrenheit, well within the range of a nasty winter. Bring all the essentials to stay warm and dry (for a list of backpacking essentials, see page 158).

Inner Canyon. Summer in the Inner Canyon is literally like playing with fire. We're talking temperatures well above 100 degrees Fahrenheit, and it doesn't take long to suffer the effects of that kind of heat. Winter conditions in the Canyon are generally a little milder than on the Rims (average 58 degrees). But that's not to say you won't get an ice storm or snowstorm once you venture below the Rim. For that reason, our pack mules are fitted with special ice shoes, and we recommend the same thing for you hikers. You can rent or buy crampons for your boots at the general store in Grand Canyon Village.

North Rim. During the winter, approximately late October through mid-May, the only access to the North Rim is by hiking, snowshoeing, or cross-country skiing. As long as you can endure the conditions (up to 150 inches of snow per year), you'll be rewarded with an uncrowd-

What is the Grand Canyon's backcountry like?

Like nothing you've ever seen. However spectacular you've imagined the Grand Canyon to be, the real thing will take your breath away.

The surrounding plateau lands—stark, wild, and elegant—are adorned with sagebrush and grasses that give the desert its distinct aroma, especially after a rain. Closer to the Canyon Rims, desert scrub mixes with pinyon-juniper woodlands and stands of ponderosa pines. On the North Rim are boreal forests of spruce, fir, and aspen. The Canyon itself remains practically hidden until you reach the edge and come face-to-face with its booming expanse of sheer cliffs and chiseled stratification.

The descent into the Canyon is a journey into an even hotter, drier world. While the temperature at the top might be 75 degrees Fahrenheit, once you reach the bottom you may be seeking shade in 105-degree weather. In this severe environment, plants adapt their shape and color to take advantage of what little moisture there is. You'll see hearty shrubs with small leaves and short stems, as if puckered against the dry, red soil. Some leaves are covered with a waxy material to seal in moisture, while others are covered with tiny gray hairs which deflect sunlight and grab moisture. Root systems are shallow, sometimes reaching into the rock crevices to brace against the wind and run-off.

Canyon animals migrate, hibernate and endure all the seasonal changes. You may see mammals and birds traveling between the Rims in search of a suitable and comfortable environment. The hottest regions host creatures who wander the nighttime hours and simply find a hole to crawl in during the day.

What should we know about camping and backpacking in Grand Canyon's backcountry?

A wilderness excursion is a bit different than a stroll through Grand Canyon Village. You should check with the nearest ranger station or visitor center for current weather and trail conditions before you embark—and then be prepared for the possibility that the forecast is completely wrong. Hiking the backcountry requires an ample amount of time for resting and setting up your campsite. The park has some suggestions and regulations that will help you enjoy your trip while preserving Grand Canyon's fragile backcountry areas.

There are 16 main trails and many small routes in the Inner Canyon, but only the corridor trails (Bright Angel and Kaibab) are maintained and checked regularly by trail crews. Remember, none of these trails is easy, not when you're dealing with such extreme elevation changes and weather conditions. Plan carefully—bring enough food and water, proper clothing, and a map and compass—and know your physical limitations. The sweltering heat has been known to disorient people and lead them to actions they might not otherwise attempt.

You must get a permit to camp anywhere in the park other than developed campgrounds on the Rims. The only exception to the rule is for those staying at Phantom Ranch (but they still need to make accommodation reservations). Backcountry permits are currently $10, plus $5 per person per night (subject to change), and can be obtained up to four months in advance through the Backcountry Information Center (see permit information in the "Quick Reference" section).

If you arrive without a permit and wish to get one, you can put your name on a waiting list by showing up at the Backcountry

Information Center at 8:00 a.m. on the day you wish to hike. Advance reservations are highly recommended. To help you plan your visit, know that the busiest times to hike the Canyon are spring, fall, and any school vacation period.

Once you get your permit and are ready to embark, remember a few helpful tips. Try to schedule at least two nights in the Canyon, so that you have a chance to rest before you hike back out. For Rim to Rim hikes, a minimum of three nights is suggested.

Hikes from the South Rim begin at 7,000 feet above sea level. You can depart from the South Rim any time of year (though you may need crampons in winter). The North Rim begins at 8,500 feet. This high altitude can cause all sorts of symptoms, like fatigue, dizziness, nausea, and headache. So take it slow at first. North Rim hiking trips can be taken from mid-May to late October.

Many species of desert plants concentrate poisonous material from the soil in their stems and leaves. The Canyon is not a good place to experiment with eating wild foods.

Do your washing and cleaning at least 100 feet from the water source (not in it!) Purify all water taken from natural sources by using iodine or bleach, or by boiling or filtering. Use toilets where provided, and bury feces at least 100 feet from trails, campsites, and water sources.

Wood or ground fires are not allowed beneath the Rims. Backpacking stoves are allowed at all campsites.

And please remember, the greatest good you can do for the Canyon is to leave no trace that you were ever here. Translation: pack out all your trash.

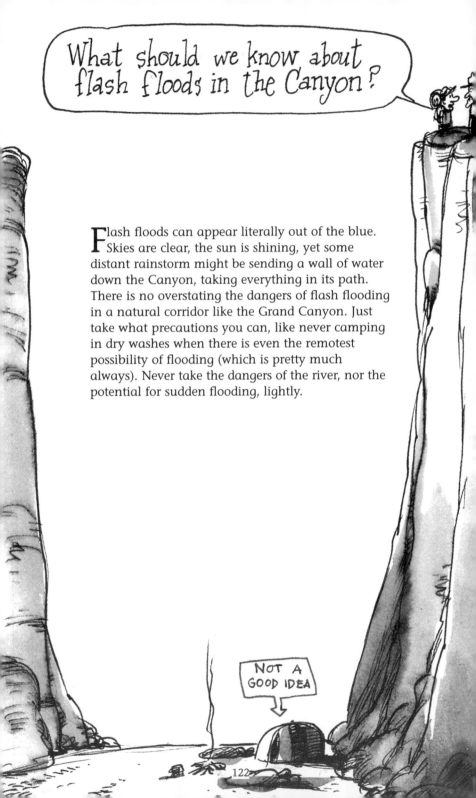

What should we know about flash floods in the Canyon?

Flash floods can appear literally out of the blue. Skies are clear, the sun is shining, yet some distant rainstorm might be sending a wall of water down the Canyon, taking everything in its path. There is no overstating the dangers of flash flooding in a natural corridor like the Grand Canyon. Just take what precautions you can, like never camping in dry washes when there is even the remotest possibility of flooding (which is pretty much always). Never take the dangers of the river, nor the potential for sudden flooding, lightly.

NOT A GOOD IDEA

WHERE IS TUWEEP?

Read it and weep: Tuweep is a remote, rugged section of wilderness near the entrance to the park's North Rim. Mohave County Road 5, a few miles west of Fredonia, is the only entrance road, and its 60 miles of graded dirt may become impassable during wet weather. There are no visitor services at Tuweep—no water, food, lodging, fuel, or transportation. Fredonia, 69 miles away, is the nearest town.

Sound like a friendly place to visit, or what? Actually, for those adventuresome enough to make the journey out here, there is a wealth of natural beauty to discover. At its elevation of 5,500 feet, Tuweep has open spaces, grass-lands, sage, and pinyon-juniper woodland. Its striking Canyon vistas reveal the history of its volcanic origins, with rounded cinder cones rising from the valley floor, remnants of ancient lava flows welded to the Canyon walls, and the astonishing sight of the Colorado River flowing 3,000 feet below.

The NPS operates a free campground that is open year-round. The sites, available on a first-come, first-served basis, have chemical toilets but no water. You may find the campground rather crowded on Memorial Day and other spring and summer weekends, but beyond that, you may have the place to yourself.

Points of interest include the Tuweep Ranger Station, which is on the National Register of Historic Places. The area offers a few great hiking trails, like Tuckup, Saddle Horse Canyon, and Lava Falls Trail. Permits for overnight hiking are required. For more information, call the Tuweep Ranger Station at (520) 716-2843.

WHERE ISSSS TUWEEEP?!!!

Will we have any problems with animals in the wilderness?

As you may have learned already in this book, the most notorious troublemakers among Grand Canyon's wildlife are squirrels and chipmunks. This holds true in the backcountry, where the little critters must have picked up a trick or two from their relatives in Grand Canyon Village.

Every year, Arizona reports cases of the bubonic plague (yes, THE plague), which can be carried by squirrels. Canyon squirrels are beggars who bite, so avoid the temptation to strike up a food exchange program when they visit your campsite. That way, you can avoid infection and a trip to the clinic for some painful shots. Also, try not to leave scraps of food or easily accessed food bags around, as they will be ambushed.

Other animals to consider are snakes and scorpions. Rattlesnakes do live in the Canyon; however, they are naturally shy animals who will bite only if surprised or extremely provoked. To avoid catching one off-guard, make some noise (screaming isn't necessary, just some foot-shuffling or whistling) when you're walking on the trail. Scorpions are easily avoided by shaking out your shoes in the morning. They like dark, warm places (we won't talk about the smell), so before you slip on those sneakers, take a second and knock them around a bit.

DANGER

BEGGARS CAN BE BITERS!

VI

Recreational Opportunities

What's there to do around here?

The Grand Canyon, the Colorado River, and the surrounding lands offer many opportunities for all types of recreation. The only wild card is the climate—hot and arid in the summer, freezing and snowy in the winter. For those who are ready for extreme weather, the area is a mecca for outdoor activities.

Walking. A leisurely walk along either the South or North Rim, with stops at museums, visitor centers, ancestral Anasazi sites, and historic structures, can be a perfect introduction to the park. There are 10 miles of maintained walking trails along the South Rim, and more than 20 miles of maintained trails along the North Rim.

Hiking. A journey on our 500 miles of rim and canyon trails (including 33 miles of maintained trails) begins with a single step. From strolls through a ponderosa pine forest along the rim, to steep descents into the canyon, our many paths take you through the Grand Canyon's most spectacular landscapes and backcountry areas. For those who want to stay close to the main visitor areas in the park, try a short jaunt on a trail below the rims.

Bicycling. For a swifter but more challenging tour, you can bike on all paved and secondary roadways along the rims from April to October. No two-wheelers are allowed on any rim or canyon trails. There are some fun gravel roads for good mountain biking in national forest lands surrounding the park. It's best if you bring your own bike, since rentals are not available in the park, and the closest shops are located in Flagstaff or Sedona, Arizona.

River Rafting and Running. Year-round, the Grand Canyon vicinity provides awesome river recreation. A one-day, smooth-water float trip along the Colorado runs from April to October, while 3- to 21-day oar- or motor-powered white-water rafting trips lure experienced river runners and visitors year-round. Be prepared for cold water temperatures and some of the world's swiftest currents. All river trips are guided by experienced and licensed outfitters (see pages 140–143).

Fishing. Some of the best fishing in the park happens at either end of the Canyon. At the western end, there's great fishing along 16 miles of the Colorado River from Lees Ferry to Lake Mead. At the western tip, Lake Mead offers good fishing and other water recreation opportunities. If you're up for a hike or mule ride, you can try your luck around Phantom Ranch, about nine miles below the South Rim (see pages 146–147). An Arizona State Fishing License is required.

Swimming. Although swimming seems like a natural activity in a place with such a big river running through it, do not try to swim in the mighty Colorado. Powerful currents and temperatures of 45–50 degrees Fahrenheit have taken many lives. You'll have better luck in some of the side streams, although cold temperatures still pose hypothermia risks. For these reasons, we generally don't encourage swimming as a recreational activity. You also won't find any swimming pools in the park.

Horseback Riding. Mule rides in the Grand Canyon have been popular since the 1890s. Riding a horse or mule into the canyon or in the surrounding forests is great fun, and there are several ways to do it: on your own or with a licensed outfitter. For milder excursions, take a one-, two-, or four-hour horseback trail ride with a wrangler/guide. These rides begin at the corrals at Moqui Lodge in Tusayan, just outside the park's south entrance, and take you through national forest lands on the South Rim (see pages 144–145).

Cross-country Skiing and Snowshoeing. Some of the park's best-kept secrets are winter activities. There's cross-country skiing through South Rim national forests and, although the North Rim area is closed following the first snow, you can try your luck skiing or snowshoeing into the park on the Jacob Lake Road (see pages 148–149).

The entire park is accessible to hikers, but unless you have the survival instincts of a chuckwalla, you have to be an expert with a map and compass to travel off-trail. When you hike the trails in the park, you're carrying on a tradition that goes back thousands of years. These trails—trekked by Indians, pioneers, and generations of backpackers and hikers—are your best shot at getting an insider's look at the Grand Canyon.

Most of the park's 1.2 million acres is dry, rugged backcountry with plenty of scenic wonders for the curious hiker. To enjoy your experience, you'll need to take responsibility for your own safety and for preserving this dynamic and fragile national park.

HERE ARE A FEW HINTS FOR GETTING THE MOST OUT OF YOUR HIKING ADVENTURE:

⇨ Begin your hike by stopping by a ranger station or visitor center for information on current trail conditions. Trails can be temporarily closed due to unexpected weather. It's best to be an informed hiker, not a disappointed one.

⇨ Allow plenty of time for your hiking adventure: at lease twice as much time to hike out as to hike in. Don't forget that the Grand Canyon is a mountain that you'll have to hike up, after your long hike down.

⇨ The terrain below the rims is a desert. Always plan to carry and drink at least one gallon of water per person per day, and eat high energy snacks often to keep up your energy. Plan your hike so you don't travel long distances without allowing adequate time to rest, cool down, and enjoy the spectacular scenery.

⇨ Except for short day hikes, always try to hike with a companion. Inform others of your plans and stick to them so you can be found in case of emergency.

⇨ Wear layered clothing, as temperatures rise during a descent into the Canyon. A waterproof cover-up will help when the weather suddenly changes. Take along some moleskin in case of blisters.

⇨ Help keep our backcountry areas clean for everyone by packing out all your trash and garbage.

Now, let's go hiking!

In the speech bubbles: "What should we take on our day hike?" "WATER!! WATER!!"

In a word, **WATER**. For any kind of walk or hike in the Grand Canyon, water is your best friend. Day hikes are fairly easy to prepare for, but backpacking trips are a whole different matter. A jaunt into the backcountry for several days will probably mean investing in some equipment and clothes.

Here's a rundown on summer day-hiking essentials. Don't pack too much, as you never want to take more than you can easily carry—especially in the heat. Start with a pair of sturdy, comfortable sneakers, lightweight hiking boots, or hiking shoes with good traction. Hiking boots are recommended for Hermit, Grandview, and other unmaintained trails. During hot summer days, a hat that keeps the sun off your head and a shirt that protects your upper body will help you maintain a safe body temperature. If you become overheated, you can cool down by pouring water on your hat and shirt. Shorts and cotton T-shirts are popular for hiking, but if the weather changes, you'll be glad to have a pair of loose pants and a shirt made of material that dries quickly, like nylon or a nylon/cotton blend; these types of clothing also layer nicely. During our cooler months and even late on a summer day, a water- and wind-proof shell with attached hood is essential in case of a sudden downpour.

A small, comfortable daypack, knapsack, or fanny pack with plenty of water is essential. In hot weather and on difficult hikes, make sure you carry one gallon of water per person—and make sure you drink it! Take along nutritious, high-energy snacks that you can munch along the way, like candy, nuts, fruit, and cheese. Whatever you bring, remember to pack out all your trash. Other essentials for your pack include a map, sunscreen, lip balm, sunglasses, and a first-aid kit (or just a few bandages to take care of any scrapes and cuts). Sometimes a hike lasts longer than you expect, so instead of having to find your way back to the rim in the dark, pack a flashlight.

Depending upon your interests, you can bring along other items that will make your adventures more interesting, such as field books, binoculars, and a camera. If you plan to hike off-trail, a compass, fire starter, signal mirror, knife, and police whistle are vital tools; just make sure you know how to use them before you embark on your hike.

What else do we need to know about hiking in the Grand Canyon?

You can usually escape the crowds by hiking the North Rim or into the canyon—anywhere away from the South Rim's main visitor areas. And while you're awestruck by one of the world's great wilderness areas, don't forget to take some basic precautions to make your hike a fun and safe experience.

Summer weather in the Grand Canyon is, at best, extremely hot and dry. When you combine the extreme heat with the ruggedness of the terrain, you get dangerous conditions that may result in heat exhaustion, dehydration, and heat stroke. It's best to plan your hike during the cooler seasons of spring or fall. If summer is your only option, try to avoid the high temperatures by following some important guidelines:

⇨ Consider hiking the rim trails, which can be about 20–30 degrees cooler than the canyon floor;

⇨ Overnight hikers into the canyon should begin their trip, their daily changes of camp, and their return hike to the rim, before 7:30 a.m. or after 4:00 p.m.;

⇨ Wear a hat, and light clothing that covers the body;

⇨ Take along clothes that you can layer; include wind- and water-resistant outer clothing;

⇨ Protect your skin and eyes from the sun; wear light but supportive footwear; and pack lightly (but don't forget safety items).

Hypothermia can be a problem when night-time temperatures dip down to freezing on the rim, or when you're wet and exhausted during windy weather conditions in the Inner Canyon. A well-prepared hiker is ready for the most unpredictable changes in weather. See "Quick Reference" for a list of hiking and backpacking supplies.

Although rattlesnake bites are rare, scorpion stings happen more frequently. Take precautions when lifting wood or rocks, shake out sleeping bags, and check boots before dressing. Avoid nests of red ants that can leave painful bites, and watch for the spines of cactus and agave plants.

Even though river and stream water may look good enough to drink, there are certain organisms that can make you regret that first gulp. Giardia and Campylobactor bacteria can cause mild to really painful intestinal distress. If you can't boil fresh water for three to five minutes, treat it with iodine or filter it (maximum effective filter pore size for Giardia is five microns).

Off-trail hiking is often hazardous to people and to the fragile vegetation and cryptogamic soils of the canyon (brown, black, or gray-colored soils covered with a mixture of algae, moss, or fungi). Try to minimize your impact on the canyon. Although sections of the canyon trails can be difficult to follow, relocate the trail, even if it means backtracking. If you're hiking in an area without a trail, try to walk on hard surfaces like bedrock, boulders, or dry washes. When choosing a lunch or camp site, use previously used sites or areas with hard surfaces, like slickrock or gravel. Use established toilets where provided, and don't put your trash in them. Remember, carry all trash out with you (including toilet paper, ash, and charcoal).

If you want to learn more about hiking in the Grand Canyon, pick up a copy of the *Official Guide to Hiking the Grand Canyon* by Scott Thybony.

We'd like an easy day hike. Any suggestions?

If you're looking for an easy trail that doesn't take you into the canyon, and takes no more than 2½ to 3 hours, the following chart will give you some suggestions. These popular hikes follow along the easier rim trails, and won't wipe you out for the rest of the day. The trailheads are easy to find, with spectacular views and scenic photo spots, some picnic areas, and plenty of ways to hop onto other good trails. All of them are good for families with children.

Although these are considered easy hikes, there's really no such thing at the Grand Canyon. High temperatures, especially during the summer months, mean you have to take precautions to avoid heat exhaustion, heat stroke, or hypothermia. Here are some hiking tips that will help:

➪ Always allow more time than you think the hike will take;

➪ Eat high-energy and salty foods frequently;

➪ Drink lots of water (at least 1 gallon per day per person) to replace fluids;

➪ Stay cool by soaking your hat and shirt at water sources;

➪ Always seek shade, and avoid hiking during the hottest part of the day (10:00 a.m.– 4:00 p.m.);

➪ Go slow, and avoid huffing and puffing by resting frequently.

For more detailed hiking information and maps refer to the hiking guides listed in "Further Reading," pages 213–214.

HIKE BY AREA	DISTANCE*	DIFFICULTY	STARTS FROM
SOUTH RIM			
Grand Canyon Village Loop	3 miles	easy	Any viewpoint in Village
Hermit Road (West Rim Drive)	8 miles	easy	West Rim Interchange
(Walk one way and return via shuttle; or just walk between any two lookout points, then take shuttle back. Shuttle may not operate year round.)			
Mather Point to Yavapai Observation Station	1 mile	easy	Mather Point
Pima Point to Hermits Rest	1.1 mile	easy	Pima Point
NORTH RIM			
Cape Royal Trail	0.5 mile	easy	Cape Royal parking lot
Bright Angel Point Trail	1 mile	easy	Grand Canyon Lodge
Transept Trail	3 miles	easy	Grand Canyon Lodge

* round trip

How about some more challenging hikes?

These main corridor trails take you over the rims and into the canyon, except where indicated. They're tougher than the easy hikes, requiring more time and a lot more *oomph* to walk up out of the canyon. Families with children are welcome to have a go; just make sure you have the time to rest often, and take along plenty of water and snacks. Many of these treks will lead you to awesome scenery, and you'll get a chance to experience the canyon as never before.

Make sure you take a look at the six hiking tips on page 132 before starting your trek. That way, you can avoid having the experience of heat exhaustion, heat stroke, and hypothermia.

For more information, refer to the hiking guides listed on pages 213–214.

HIKE BY AREA	DISTANCE*	DIFFICULTY	STARTS FROM
SOUTH RIM			
Bright Angel Trail to 1.5-Mile Resthouse	3 miles	moderate	Bright Angel Trailhead
South Kaibab Trail to Cedar Ridge	3 miles	moderate +	South Kaibab Trailhead
Bright Angel Trail to 3-Mile Resthouse	6 miles	moderate +	Bright Angel Trailhead
Bright Angel Trail to Indian Garden	9.2 miles	moderate +	Bright Angel Trailhead
NORTH RIM			
North Kaibab Trail to Supai Tunnel	4 miles	moderate +	North Kaibab Trailhead
North Kaibab Trail to Roaring Springs	9.4 miles	moderate +	North Kaibab Trailhead
Uncle Jim Trail	10 miles	moderate (rim)	Ken Patrick Trail off North Kaibab Trailhead
Widforss Trail	10 miles	moderate (rim)	Widforss Trailhead (2 miles north of lodge)

*round trip

What are some great butt-kicking hikes?

For those who like to get their hearts really pumping and feel the burn in their legs, here's a list of some strenuous wilderness trails that will happily oblige. You'll need to be in good shape and carefully plan your trip for these babies, but they'll pay you back with some spectacular scenery, and a feeling of accomplishment once you're finished. All of these require multi-day trips (two to three days), and many have overnight backcountry camping sites along the way. Just be sure you have the time, conditioning, and energy before embarking on these journeys, as all of them of them have strenuous uphill climbs.

Don't forget to take a look at the hiking tips on page 132, and it's probably a good idea to refer to the "Camping and Backpacking" section of this book. For more information on other hikes in the Canyon, pick up a copy of the *Official Guide to Hiking the Grand Canyon* by Scott Thybony or *Grand Canyon Loop Hikes* by George Steck.

You gotta be kiddin' me!

HIKE BY AREA	DISTANCE*	DIFFICULTY	STARTS FROM
SOUTH RIM			
Bright Angel Trail to Plateau Point	12.2 miles	strenuous	Bright Angel Trailhead
Bright Angel Trail to Bright Angel Campground	18.6 miles	strenuous	Bright Angel Trailhead
Bright Angel Trail Phantom Ranch	19.6 miles	strenuous	Bright Angel Trailhead
South Kaibab Trail to Phantom Ranch	13.8 miles	strenuous	South Kaibab Trailhead
INNER CANYON			
South Rim to North Rim	42 miles	strenuous	South or North Kaibab Trailheads
NORTH RIM			
Ken Patrick Trail	20 miles	moderately strenuous	North Kaibab Trailhead parking lot
North Kaibab Trail to Ribbon Falls	16.8 miles	strenuous	North Kaibab Trailhead
North Kaibab Trail to Phantom Ranch	28 miles	strenuous	North Kaibab Trailhead
North Kaibab Trail to Bright Angel Campground	29 miles	strenuous	North Kaibab Trailhead
WESTERN GRAND CANYON			
Hualapai Hilltop to Supai Village	16 miles	strenuous	Hualapai Hilltop

*round trip

Can We mountain bike in Grand Canyon?

The good news for mountain bikers is that you can ride on all paved and secondary roadways and portions of the greenway scheduled for construction in 2000. The bad news is that none of the roads are well-suited for mountain biking, and the traffic along the South Rim can be a biking nightmare. All park trails, off-road backcountry areas, service roads, and utility corridors are off-limits to two-wheelers. There are numerous backcountry roads in the Kaibab National Forest around both the North and South Rims that lend themselves to both mountain biking and bike touring.

Unless an early snowstorm closes the roadways, your window for biking opportunities lasts from May through October around the North Rim; the busy South Rim offers year-round biking, but fewer options. The best time to ride in the national forestlands surrounding the park is during the clear, cooler days of September and October, when traffic is lighter (especially on the North Rim).

The park's shoulderless roads can be a challenge for novice bikers. Add some snow and icy conditions in the spring, and it can be downright dangerous. Other hazards include heavy summer traffic, which usually results in at least a few bike-versus-car accidents each year. It's best to avoid peak traffic periods (mid-morning to late afternoon during our summer months) on the roads that serve the main points of interest in the park. Riding at the crack of dawn or in the late afternoon in the forests surrounding the North Rim can be awesome.

Guided mountain bike tours led by knowledgeable guides are offered by a variety of companies, and cater to most ability levels. Depending on the company, tours usually provide a

Uh... no.

138

mountain bike, helmet, water bottle, and instruction in biking techniques and trail etiquette. For a list of licensed bicycle outfitting companies, refer to the "Quick Reference" section of this book.

Repair services and bicycle rentals are available in the Arizona communities of Flagstaff (80 miles from the park's south entrance) and Sedona (110 miles from the park's south entrance). Prices range from $20 to $25 for a full-day rental, and $15 to $18 for a half-day rental. Some shops include helmets, tool kits, and water bottles, but it's best to ask. Refer to the telephone directory in the "Quick Reference Section" for a list of bicycle rental and repair shops.

BEFORE YOU RIDE OFF INTO THE DISTANCE, HERE ARE A FEW RULES AND SAFETY PRECAUTIONS:

- ➪ Bicycle riders on public roadways in Grand Canyon National Park must obey the same rules and regulations that apply to motorized vehicles.
- ➪ Bicycles are not allowed on any park trails or in off-road backcountry areas. Service roads and utility corridors are closed to bikes unless use is expressly permitted.
- ➪ Bicycles must exhibit a white light in front and a red light or reflector on the rear during periods of low visibility.
- ➪ Wear a helmet and high-visibility clothing.
- ➪ Ride single file. Riding abreast on a public roadway is prohibited.
- ➪ Pull over and allow motorists to pass if you are impeding traffic flow.
- ➪ Yield the right-of-way to hikers and horse riders if you encounter them.
- ➪ The maximum number of cyclists traveling in a single cluster may not exceed 15, and these clusters must be at least one-half mile apart.

Can we go on a river trip through the Canyon?

Absolutely. You'll be able to choose from a lot of options, including cruising speed and length of trip, but no matter how you tailor your journey along the river, you'll get a unique view of the one and only Grand Canyon. If you're looking for more relaxation than adventure, try the smooth-water raft trips that depart from Moqui Lodge by motorcoach daily, April through October. These trips make stops along Desert View (East Rim) Drive and the Cameron Trading Post on the Navajo Indian Reservation. You'll float through Glen Canyon on the Colorado River for 4 to 5 hours, from Glen Canyon Dam near Page, Arizona, to Lees Ferry, Arizona. The trip includes a leisurely picnic on the river. Half-day and full-day trips are available. For reservations and information, call Moqui Lodge at (520) 638-2424 (for bus and raft trip), or (520) 645-3279 (for raft trip only).

For the more adventuresome, there are many commercial river concessionaires that take visitors on white-water rafting expeditions down the Colorado in the Grand Canyon. Trips vary in length from 3 days to 3 weeks. All embark from Lees Ferry, with the option of taking a partial trip starting or ending at Phantom Ranch. Some trips are motorized, and others are oar-powered. They run from April to October. Rates vary depending upon length of trip and transportation costs. All equipment, facilities, and meals are provided. Keep an eye out for the occasional reduced rates for families, children, groups, and off-season travel.

For a list of the river companies, with addresses and telephone numbers, refer to the "Quick Reference" section of this book. Due to their popularity, you'll need to make reservations for these trips well in advance.

What do we need to know about white-water rafting down the Colorado in the park?

The first thing to know is that the stretch of the Colorado River that winds through the Grand Canyon offers some of the best white-water rafting opportunities and guided rafting trips in the world. Almost anyone, including those who are physically challenged, can take one of these trips.

All the river-rafting companies who lead trips on the Colorado have experienced guides, so don't worry if you don't have prior river experience. However, the rigors of outdoor life are not for everyone. There are inherent risks, and medical help is not readily available. Still, the safety records of our registered outfitters are excellent, and guides are well-trained in first-aid and evacuation techniques. Since everyone wears a Coast Guard-approved life jacket, there is little chance of trouble should you fall in the river. While swimming ability is recommended, many non-swimmers take these trips each year.

On most of the trips, you're on the raft from four to eight hours a day. Trip itineraries usually include daily stops at beaches, scenic side canyons, and points of interest, with many opportunities to hike, swim, and just relax. Each day, your guides will set up camp, complete with a kitchen and portable toilet. Good hearty meals (some companies offer vegetarian) are included.

Depending upon the time of year, camping along the river has many benefits; the weather is warmer, and there are fewer insects. The best months for rafting through the Grand Canyon are May, September, and October, when the average high temperature is 82 degrees Fahrenheit, and the average low is 57 degrees. During the spring and fall, it may feel like you have the river to yourselves (a "no-motors" period begins after September 15). During June, July, and August, daytime temperatures frequently exceed 100 degrees, although the humidity is low and there is a natural cooling effect while on the river. Expect rain any month, though afternoon thunder showers are most likely July through mid-September.

While you're on the Colorado River, you may see some experienced river runners (besides your guides). You can have a great time watching them go down the big "Class 10" rapids (most other rivers have "Class 5" rapids).

Refer to the "Quick Reference" section in this book for a list of whitewater rafting companies. Remember, a visit to websites can be very informative. When you make your reservations, be sure to ask about what is and isn't included in the trip, as that can vary from company to company.

THE COLORADO RIVER THROUGH THE GRAND CANYON: WORLD-CLASS RIVER RUNNING

RIVER FACTS

Length: 277 river miles through the Canyon
Average width: 300 feet
Minimum width: 75 feet at Middle Granite Gorge (river mile 135)
Average depth: 40 feet
Greatest depth: 85 feet
Average gradient: 8 feet per mile
Elevation of river:
> Lees Ferry (east end of Canyon): 3,116 feet
> Lake Mead (west end of Canyon): 1,200 feet

Average annual precipitation:
> Lees Ferry: 5.8 inches
> Lake Mead: 4.6 inches
> Phantom Ranch: 8.4 inches (historically, ranges between 3–15 inches)

John Wesley Powell was the first explorer to go through the Canyon on the Colorado River, back in 1869. Most of the points along the river were named by Powell. The following are some of the most difficult rapids along the 277-mile stretch of the river in the Canyon (approximate river mile indicated):

Badger Creek Rapid (Mile 8)	Ruby Rapid (Mile 105)
House Rock Rapid (Mile 17)	Serpentine Rapid (Mile 106)
North Canyon Rapid (Mile 20)	Waltenberg Rapid (Mile 112)
24 and 25 Mile Rapid	Specter Rapid (Mile 129)
Cave Springs Rapid (Mile 25)	Bedrock Rapid (Mile 130)
Kwagunt Rapid (Mile 56)	Deubendorff Rapid (Mile 132)
Unkar Rapid (Mile72)	Tapeats Rapid (Mile 134)
Hance Rapid (Mile 77)	Upset Rapid (Mile 150)
Sockdolager Rapid (Mile 79)	Lava Falls Rapid (Mile 179)
Zoroaster Rapid (Mile 84)	Kolb Rapid (Mile 205)
Horn Creek Rapid (Mile 90)	209 Mile Rapid
Granite Rapid (Mile 93)	Little Bastard Rapid (Mile 212)
Hermit Rapid (Mile 95)	

RIVER RUNNING ON THE COLORADO

- The first solo river-running trip down the Colorado in the Canyon was made in 1937, with the first inflatable boat trip and commercial trip made in 1938. The first motorized run down the Colorado in the Canyon was accomplished in 1949.

- The best place to watch river runners rigging their boats is Lees Ferry.

- Commercial river guides are usually friendly and don't mind answering a few questions.

- The waiting list is years-long for private river-running trips through the Grand Canyon. To add your name, write to: The River District Office, Grand Canyon National Park, P.O. Box 129, Grand Canyon, AZ 86023.

Can we go horseback riding?

High in the saddle, you can get a unique perspective of the Grand Canyon and surrounding lands without ever breaking a sweat. You'll also be part of a long park tradition, as virtually all of the early exploration of the Grand Canyon was done on horseback. There are no horseback trail rides inside park boundaries (for mule trips in the park, refer to pages 82–83 in "Getting Around"). However, there are several stables just outside the park that lead guided rides through forests and along both Canyon Rims.

South Rim. One- or two-hour rides and half-day (four-hour) trail rides are offered by Apache Stables. These stables are located at Moqui Lodge, in Kaibab National Forest on Highway 64, just outside the south entrance to the park. These unforgettable rides take you along trails that wander through the ponderosa pines of Kaibab National Forest. The half-day ride is the most popular, and follows a trail east through Long Jim Canyon to a spectacular rim view of the Grand Canyon. Cost is $25 for the one-hour ride (offered year-round), $40 for the two-hour ride (May–November), and $65 for the half-day ride (May–November). From May until the first cold spell in late fall, these stables also offer twilight campfire trail rides as well as wagon rides. These rides include a one-hour evening amble on a horse or a horse-drawn wagon, ending with a western campfire (all return by wagon). Costs are $30 for the trail/wagon ride, and $8.50 for just the wagon ride. Reserve well in advance by calling (520) 638-2891 or (520) 638-2424. You can also write Apache Stables, P.O. Box 158, Grand Canyon, AZ 86023, or visit them online at www.apachestables.com.

North Rim. From May to October, you can join one- or two-hour, half-day (four-hour), or full-day trail rides with Allen's Trail Rides. It's located in Kaibab National Forest on Highway 67, just outside the north entrance to the park. These rides take you through the ponderosa pines of Kaibab National Forest surrounding the North Rim. The full-day ride takes you along the historic Arizona Trail and the

Canyon Rim. Cost is $20 for the one-hour ride, $35 for the two-hour ride, $55 for the half-day ride, and $85 for the full-day ride, which includes lunch along the trail. Year-round, there are custom pack trips that cost $100/day per person, including three meals. All of these rides require advance reservations. Call (435) 644-8150.

Western Grand Canyon (outside park boundaries). If you have at least three days, you can try a saddle and packhorse trip into one of the most remote and beautiful corners of the southwestern part of the Grand Canyon. The trail starts at Hualapai Hilltop, 66 miles from Peach Springs on old Highway 66. You'll ride eight miles through stunning Canyon scenery along Havasu Canyon Trail, to the Indian village of Supai on the Havasupai Indian Reservation. Here you'll find lodging and food services, as well as some of the Canyon's most beautiful waterfalls, which I've described on pages 36–37. The cost of the saddle and packhorse trip from the Hualapai Hilltop Trailhead to the Village of Supai and back is $80. The cost of a round trip from the trailhead to the campground, which is located two miles below Supai Village, is $110 (packhorses carry all equipment). For more information, call the Havasupai Tourist Office at (520) 448-2121 or the Havasupai Lodge at (520) 448-2111. The lodge also offers day-time guided trail rides to Havasu Falls for $45 per person. Call the Havasupai Lodge for more information.

Forget about hiking. Some of the best trout fishing in the country, complete with easy boat access, is located at Lees Ferry, at the park's northeastern boundary. The more adventuresome can try a long hike down the Canyon or a raft trip down the Colorado to one of many small tributary streams. At the western boundary of the park, on the Hualapai Indian Reservation, you'll find more good fishing by boat in the Lower Granite Gorge and Lake Mead areas.

Although fishing in the Grand Canyon can be done all year long, the best time of year is generally during the fall and winter. During those seasons, there are fewer people, cooler weather, and lower water levels at Glen Canyon Dam.

Anglers 14 years and older are required to have an Arizona fishing license. You can purchase one at the Delaware North Park Services store (formerly Babbitt's General Store) in Grand Canyon Village on the South Rim, or at Marble Canyon Lodge near Lees Ferry. You'll also need a backcountry use permit for any overnight hiking or rafting jaunts into the Canyon. The cost of the license varies. If you're a non-resident of Arizona, you can get a five-day permit for $18.50, a one-day license for $8, or an annual non-resident license for $48, including a trout stamp. If you're an Arizona resident, you'll pay $22 for a license with a trout stamp.

Along with ensuring a fun and fruitful fishing trip for you, the park's fishing regulations are crucial to the Grand Canyon's ecosystem. For instance, along the 16-mile stretch of prime fishing habitat from Lees Ferry to Glen Canyon, anglers are only allowed to fish with barbless hooks, flies, and lures; no bait allowed. We also have strict limit regulations that allow each angler to catch and keep two fish a day that measure under 16 inches. Any fish over 16 inches must be returned to the river unharmed to help encourage a bigger-size fish population.

Where are the best fishing spots?

Let's take a look at the options you have for fishing the waters of the Grand Canyon.

(eastern end of Grand Canyon). Some of the best fishing at the Grand Canyon is along the 16-mile stretch of the Colorado River between Lees Ferry and Glen Canyon. More than half of the park's landed fish are caught here. Lees Ferry is accessible by paved road off Highway 89A, and is located 84 miles from the park's north entrance and 127 miles from its south entrance. There are two fishing outfitters who can get you on the river. Located near Lees Ferry, Marble Canyon Lodge provides anglers with guides, boats, and fishing equipment. Call them at (520) 355-2225. Lees Ferry Anglers is a complete fishing outfitter, offering day trips that include guides, boats, fuel, and lunch. You'll be taken to some of the best fishing holes along this stretch of the river, and get tips on catching the area's most plentiful species of trout: the rainbow (some measure close to 24 inches). The cost is $250 for one person, $300 for two people, and $400 for three people, with a maximum of three anglers per boat. Call Lees Ferry Anglers at (520) 355-2261 for more information. There are some pretty strict regulations for fishing along this stretch of the Colorado. Check with the Backcountry Information Center for more information at (520) 638-7875.

(Inner Canyon). To get to the fishing holes around Phantom Ranch you'll have to hike or take a mule ride down Bright Angel Trail. Once you're at the Ranch you'll have lots of opportunities for a chance at a rainbow, as you dip your line in Bright Angel Creek or the Colorado River. Some basic fishing supplies are available for guests of the Ranch. All you need to bring is your own pole, reel, and maybe some bait. Call Grand Canyon National Park Lodges for more information at (520) 638-2631.

(western end of the Grand Canyon). At the opposite end of the Colorado River from Lees Ferry, Lake Mead offers an unparalled area for water recreation and fishing. There are various marinas on the lake that rent boats, but you'll have to be your own guide. There's a public boat ramp at Meadview which provides easy access to fishing in the lower Grand Canyon. For more information about this area, call the Pierce Ferry Campground and Ranger Station at Lake Mead National Recreation Area, at (520) 767-3401.

Winter in the Grand Canyon is a study in contrasts. While the roads to the South Rim remain open, the North Rim road is closed to all automobile traffic. You can enjoy cross-country skiing and snowshoeing along both the North Rim (most of the winter) and the South Rim (when there's enough snow). Inside the Canyon you'll be treated to mild hiking weather and relatively empty trails and campgrounds. Visitors to the South Rim can enjoy all park programs including guided walks, talks, hikes, and tours (weather permitting), while the only way to access and enjoy the North Rim is via cross-country skis or snowshoes.

Whether you can cross-country ski or snowshoe on the South Rim during the winter depends on how much snow there is. Conditions permitting, you can rent skis at the Delaware North Park Services stores in Tusayan and Grand Canyon Village (formerly Babbitt's General Stores). You'll find groomed trails in the Kaibab National Forest near the Arizona Trail, east of Grandview Point. For hardy campers, Mather Campground stays open all year. For more information, call the visitor center at (520) 638-7888 or the Tusayan Ranger District Office at (520) 638-2443.

Winter inside the Canyon is one of the park's best-kept secrets, a real treat for the more adventuresome visitors. Although you may have to gear up by adding crampons to your boots as you hike down ice- or snow-covered trails, once you're inside the Canyon the weather is mild, the trails are empty, and the camping superb. Between November and March, reservations for a mule trip down to Phantom Ranch are easier to get, and the weather isn't as hot. Call Grand Canyon National Park Lodges for advance reservations at (303) 29-PARKS. For an unforgettable backpacking experience, you can camp at any of the backcountry campgrounds inside the Canyon.

The North Rim is a winter wonderland. While snow is usually plentiful, services are not. After the road to the North Rim closes with the first snow, you won't find any water, toilet, or other services except in Jacob Lake, 32 miles north of the park entrance. If you're still willing to give it a shot, you'll need to get a backcountry permit—call (520) 638-7875—and be conditioned for long-distance skiing. The Jacob Lake Campground is open, minus any facilities. Remember, snowmobiles are not allowed inside park boundaries. Call the North Rim Ranger Office for more information at (520) 638-7888. There's also cross-country skiing throughout the Kaibab National Forest lands around the North Rim. Call the North Kaibab Ranger District Office in Fredonia, Arizona at (520) 643-7395. The office is staffed year-round. You can also arrange your own winter pack trip on horseback with Allen's Trail Rides. Call them at (435) 644-8150.

·The Future of the Grand Canyon·

As a world heritage site, the Grand Canyon is recognized as a place of universal value, containing natural and cultural features that should be preserved as part of the heritage of all people. Because it is one of the most popular national park sites in the world, it has become increasingly difficult to control the impact created by five million annual visitors and their cars on the few developed areas along the Rims. This is especially true of the South Rim, where most of the visitation in the park occurs. The roads and facilities were never designed to handle this volume of use, resulting in a gradual degradation of the visitor experience and negative impacts on the park's natural and cultural resources.

Over the next three to five years, the National Park Service will work with many private, state, and federal agencies to implement an ambitious regional plan that will make many changes to both the North and South Rims of the Grand Canyon. This plan will not only fulfill the NPS mission to protect and preserve park resources, but will also greatly improve the visitor experience of the park.

The first change will be in the form of a proposed new 272-acre commercial development in the town of Tusayan, located in Kaibab National Forest just outside the south entrance to the park. The Canyon Forest Village project will be built by a private development company and will encompass 20 acres of housing for park employees, new hotels, restaurants, and other amenities.

There will be a light rail system which will run from a new Grand Canyon Transit Center in Tusayan to designated points within Grand Canyon Village. A parking lot to accommodate day-use visitors to the South Rim will be located adjacent to the Canyon Forest Village development. Water for the development will be transported from the Colorado River, rather than from within the Canyon.

Inside the park, changes will include increasing emphasis on alternative forms of transportation, including public transit, hiking, and biking. A new Canyon View Information Plaza will be built at Mather Point. This visitor orientation center will be the central transit center for the South Rim. It will be the primary point for continuous direct connections to Grand Canyon Village and Hermit Road (formerly West Rim Drive), the Yaki Point trailhead, or the transit center in Tusayan. The Canyon View center will include a transit pick-up and drop-off area, covered shelter and seating, information and display panels, and restrooms. Walking trails, bike paths, and bicycle rentals will be available. There will be no parking lot at Canyon View. Visitors will have to park their vehicles in Tusayan, and take public transit service into the park.

South Rim. Here are some additional changes planned for the South Rim:

➪ Electronic message signs south of Tusayan and in Cameron will advise travelers about the status of parking on the South Rim;

➪ Access to East Rim overlooks will be restricted;

➪ Overnight guests will be allowed to drive to the designated parking areas for their lodging. Tour buses with overnight guests will be allowed direct access to lodging units to drop off passengers;

➪ A smaller orientation and transportation center will be built at Desert View, where visitor services will be moved farther back from the Rim;

➪ New interpretive exhibits along the South Rim will be built, and an outdoor exhibit will be provided at Yavapai Observation Station;

➪ New interpretive exhibits of the traditional and contemporary relationships between American Indians and the Grand Canyon will be located throughout the park;

➪ Hermits Rest, Lookout Studio, and the Desert View Watchtower will be converted back to their original uses, and the gift shops will be reduced in size.

North Rim. On the North Rim, visitors can expect some of the following changes, made in an attempt to maintain a low-key, uncrowded atmosphere:

⇨ A day-visitor reservation system will be implemented when visitation warrants it, so that visitor use can be better distributed on Bright Angel Point, and more visitors will be encouraged to visit Walhalla Plateau;

⇨ Private vehicle use on Bright Angel Point will be restricted, transit service will be introduced, and bike and pedestrian pathways will be expanded on the point and Walhalla Plateau;

⇨ Visitors will receive information about the North Rim outside the park at the U.S. Forest Service's Kaibab Plateau Visitor Center in Jacob Lake, and also at an orientation center on Bright Angel Point;

⇨ Lodging will be expanded by 25% by adapting existing structures;

⇨ A few campsites may be removed as part of a redesign of the campground.

The Grand Canyon begins the new century armed with a new plan to improve the quality of each visitor's experience, and to preserve the essential wildness of the Grand Canyon as a gift for all to cherish and protect. For more information on these changes visit the following websites: www.nps.gov/grca/transit or www.nps.gov/grca/future.htm.

· Ranger's Farewell ·

I hope that I've answered all of your questions about the Grand Canyon, and that you've learned some inside information on ways to make your visit to the Canyon more enjoyable.

The next section in the book is called "Quick Reference." It's filled with lots of easy-to-find facts, forms, and information about the Canyon. The subjects are in alphabetical order so you can quickly find what you need without having to thumb through the whole handbook. My favorite is a Grand Canyon time line that answers questions that we may not have covered in the rest of the book.

Good hunting, and be sure to let us know if we need to change anything to improve future versions of this handbook. You can write to me, or to Susan and Phil Frank, c/o Pomegranate, Box 6099, Rohnert Park, CA 94927.

Bye for now,

Ranger Jack

Quick Reference

National Park is the centerpiece of four major nation-
l recreation areas, including (from north to south)
tional Park, Glen Canyon National Recreation Area,
...yon National Park, and Lake Mead National Recreation
Area. Together, they stretch across some 400 miles, as the raven flies,
of the most remote and beautiful wildlands in the world, and over
800 miles along the mighty Colorado River. There are also five tribes,
or nations, of American Indians that have reservations near Grand
Canyon National Park. In other words, you'll be visiting an area rich
in natural wonders and cultural treasures. To get the most out of
your trip, you might want to visit some of the following area attractions. Refer to the telephone directory on pages 207–208 for contact
numbers.

The Arboretum at Flagstaff. Here you'll see over 200 acres of diverse
plants, all native to Northern Arizona. As you walk through the center, you'll learn about the area's native, experimental, and exotic
plant species, and their uses.

Canyon de Chelly National Monument. Visit ancient Indian ruins
from the Great Pueblo period, and see sheer sandstone walls that
soar a thousand feet into the air to create amazing vistas.

Lake Powell and Glen Canyon Dam. A national recreation area
covering over 1,800 square miles of natural beauty, Glen Canyon
Dam lies near Page, Arizona, at the border of Northern Arizona and
Utah. Take a self-guided tour of the dam, or enjoy all forms
of water recreation along the 186-mile-long Lake Powell.

Lowell Observatory, Flagstaff. Founded in 1894, this observatory
has become one of the country's leading astronomical institutions,
offering some of the clearest viewing fields in North America. Maybe
that's why the first observations of Mars were made here, leading to
the discovery of the planet Pluto in 1930.

Meteor Crater. This enormous crater measures nearly a mile wide
and over 550 feet deep, and closely resembles the surface of the
moon. The crater is a NASA-designated training ground used by
United States astronauts. Visit the Astronaut Hall of Fame and the
Museum of Astrology to learn more about this unique site.

Montezuma Castle National Monument. Located in Verde Valley,
just off Interstate 17, this national monument features one of the best
preserved cliff dwellings in the country. Explore the five-story, nine-
teen-room ruin and Montezuma's Well.

Monument Valley Navajo Tribal Park. Located near the Utah border, Monument Valley is best known for the dramatic landscape of dunes, sandstone spires, and buttes that has been the backdrop for countless Hollywood films. Take a Harveycar Tour to see this popular example of southwestern geography, and to learn more about the Navajo culture.

Museum of Northern Arizona, Flagstaff. A visit to the Grand Canyon wouldn't be complete without a visit to this museum, which features the most extensive Native American art and artifacts in the country. Located on Highway 180 just north of Flagstaff, it offers exhibits that explore all facets of the fascinating Southwest Indian cultures.

Oak Creek Canyon, Sedona. This area has become a vacation haven for visitors from across the country. Discover the dramatic scenery of red rock landscapes, and the treasures of Sedona, including art galleries, golf courses, and lots of outdoor recreational activities.

Sunset Crater and Wupatki National Monuments. The site of an ancient Anasazi ruin, Wupatki reveals secrets about the unique culture that thrived in the area for over 150 years. Located just ten minutes away, Sunset Crater is a lava flow frozen in time, from an eruption that took place some 900 years ago. You can visit both sites together on a Harveycar Tour, offered from the South Rim of the Grand Canyon.

Tuzigoot Ruin National Monument. Located near Cottonwood, Arizona, this village site is believed to have been abandoned by Native Americans sometime around 1400 A.D.

Walnut Canyon National Monument. An intricately built and well-preserved example of some 300 small cliff rooms built into the canyon's limestone walls. Located just outside Flagstaff, this is a great place to see ruins that are relatively close to a trail. Accessible by Harveycar Tour from the South Rim of the Grand Canyon.

CLOTHES
Sturdy hiking shoes or lightweight boots
Thick hiking socks
Shorts, jeans, fleece pants and sweatshirt
Cotton t-shirt or long-sleeved shirt
Rain-resistant jacket, poncho, and pants
Warm hat and gloves
Set of extra clothes (t-shirt, a long-sleeved cotton shirt, a down vest
    or light jacket)
UV protection sunglasses

EQUIPMENT
Rain-resistant sleeping bag and pad
Backpacking tent and stakes
Frame backpack (for longer hikes and overnight trips)
Flashlight/headlamp (carry fresh alkaline cells and a spare bulb)
Water bottle (at least quart-size)
Backpacking stove and fuel
Cooking pot, cup, and utensils
Fire starter kit (waterproof matches in waterproof container, candle,
    and dry paper)
Topographical map and compass
Pocket knife
Watch
Water purification device

SUPPLIES
Water (at least one gallon per person per day)
Sunscreen, insect repellant, lip balm
Small first-aid kit with blister kit
Toilet items
Food (also carry emergency rations like raisins, nuts,
    hard candy, etc.)
Miscellaneous (large bandana, extra ziplock bags)

A.D. 1–700: The earliest farmers were the ancestral Pueblo people, or Anasazi, from a Navajo word meaning "Ancient Ones." This term included both the Basketmakers and Pueblo Indians. The Basketmakers were so called because of the variety of beautiful, well-made baskets that they produced, using twisted and coiled grass and yucca leaves. By A.D. 600, the Basketmakers had learned to make pottery, baked for durability.

700: Major changes occurred in the Basketmaker way of life. Pueblo villages were independent, like Greek city-states. Rules and customs became highly developed. Reflecting their agricultural way of life, the Pueblos' religion sought rain in a dry land, and fertility for life-sustaining crops. Elaborate ceremonies included masked and costumed dancers. With pictographs and murals, they decorated the walls of *kivas* (special rooms for religious purposes), caves, and cliffs.

1000–1100: Pueblo occupation of the Grand Canyon area accelerated until there were hundreds of inhabited sites on the plateaus and in nooks and crannies of the Canyon, from rims to river. During this time, the Canyon was home to the most extensive human population in its entire history.

600–1150: The Coconino Plateau, Havasu Canyon, and parts of the Grand Canyon south of the river were occupied by an agricultural and hunting people called Cohonina. This early culture flourished in the area until its disappearance around 1150, near the time of Pueblo abandonment.

1000–1400: The Apaches and the Navajos (then closely associated peoples) migrated southward across mountains and plains. They came as nomads, hunting and raiding. Finally they settled near the Pueblo Indians, and raided them at times.

1150 to 1200: Pueblo Indians abandoned the Grand Canyon almost totally.

1540: White men saw the Grand Canyon for the first time. The discovery was an incident in the search for the Seven Cities of Cibola by Francisco Vásquez de Coronado. García López de Cárdenas, a young soldier in the expedition, is recognized as the Spanish discoverer of the Grand Canyon. The place where Cárdenas and his men first saw the Grand Canyon is not known. The point that best fits his description is the area between Moran Point and Desert View.

1776: Francisco Garces was a missionary who searched for new Indian tribes in order to win their allegiance for his Church and king. On June 20, 1776, he came into the deep canyon of the "Rio Jabesua" (Havasu, or Cataract Creek). Garces was the first writer to refer consistently to the "Rio Colorado," and named the Grand Canyon "Puerto de Bucareli". He set out for the Hopi pueblos on June 25, 1776. On the following day, he viewed the Grand Canyon, which he perceived as an endless series of canyons, within which flowed the "Rio Colorado" (Red River).

1803: With the Louisiana Purchase, the young United States of America became the northeastern neighbor of New Spain.

1821–1848: The Grand Canyon was within the territory of an independent Mexico.

1824: While still part of Mexico, the Grand Canyon was first visited by men from the United States. There was very little Mexican supervision in the canyon and plateau country around the Grand Canyon, so mountain men traveled there pretty much as they pleased, searching for beaver and other furs.

1825: William Henry Ashley, one of the leading fur traders, descended the upper Green River through several of its canyons, distinguishing himself and his six men as the first to attempt a boat trip down the Colorado's "mainstream."

1848: The Grand Canyon region became United States territory as a result of the Mexican War, which was ended by the treaty of Guadalupe Hidalgo, ratified on May 30, 1848. Also in 1848, gold was discovered in California, providing the impetus for increased travel along routes to the gold fields, passing both north and south of the Grand Canyon.

1850: The Territory of New Mexico, which included Arizona and the Grand Canyon, was created.

1857: The War Department authorized Lieutenant Joseph Christmas Ives to explore the Colorado River "to ascertain how far the river was navigable for steamboats." The expedition's artists, F. W. von Egloffstein and H. B. Mollhausen, were the first to sketch the Grand Canyon, although their sketches appear dark and forbidding, and fail to convey an impression of its beauty. Dr. John Strong Newberry, a geologist, also accompanied the expedition and had the honor of being the first scientist to study Grand Canyon, "the most splendid exposure of stratified rocks that there is in the world."

1863: Abraham Lincoln signed the bill establishing Arizona Territory.

1867 (approximate date): The Navajos signed a peace treaty with the United States, and were allowed to return to their traditional lands. The reservation then established was later expanded to include sections of the eastern Grand Canyon in 1884, 1900, and 1930.

1868: The first map containing "Grand Canyon" as a place name accompanied General William J. Palmer's railroad survey report.

1869: The Hualapais made peace with the U.S. Army, and many of their warriors served as scouts for General George Crook in his campaign against their traditional enemies, the Yavapais.

1869: Major John Wesley Powell began his exploration of the Grand Canyon. He played a leading role in the second "opening" of the West—its opening to science, conservation, and coherent use. When he completed his work, the Colorado River's path was known, its vast canyons named and measured, their ancient book of geology laid open for scientific study, and the civilization of the Indian inhabitants, ancient and modern, recorded for posterity. Powell's expedition came upon the mouth of a clear, cold stream. He named it Bright Angel. The honor of the first consistent and authoritative use of the name "Grand Canyon" belongs to Major Powell, whose definitive and widely read reports caused the name to be adopted permanently.

1870: Powell explored the plateaus north of the Grand Canyon to locate supply routes for his second river expedition.

1870–1880: Copper mining districts were opened near the Grand Canyon, in the Grand Wash Cliffs and Mt. Trumbull areas. In order to provide themselves with a supply of pack animals (burros are not native to America), prospectors released burros into the Canyon, where they thrived on the sparse vegetation and multiplied. Although some burros were lost, the population increased until, in modern times, it reached an estimated two thousand. Much destruction of plant cover and fouling of springs resulted.

1870–1890: Ranchers, settlers, and colonists arrived in the Grand Canyon region. Arizona Territory quadrupled its non-Indian population, from under 10,000 to over 40,000, and more than doubled it again, to 88,000 by 1890. In that year the U.S. Bureau of the Census declared the frontier at an end.

1871: Powell's second Colorado River expedition left Green River, Wyoming. John Doyle Lee, a controversial Mormon, moved to the crossing of the Colorado River at the mouth of the Paria River. He established a ferry there, and it has been called Lees Ferry ever since.

1872: Powell's second expedition resumed their river trip from Lees Ferry and ended at Kanab Creek. During that summer, Powell explored the Kaibab Plateau and the North Rim of the Grand Canyon.

1873: With a new boat called the Colorado, Lee instituted regular ferry business, with a charge of three dollars per wagon and seventy-five cents per animal.

1874: Most of the Hualapais were removed to a reservation on the lower Colorado River, but the Havasupais and the plateau tribes near the Grand Canyon remained.

1880: A proclamation by President Rutherford B. Hayes established the Havasupai Indian Reservation. This area, which was 5 miles wide and 12 miles long, surrounded the village and the cultivated portion of the canyon.

1880–1881: Clarence Edward Dutton of the new United States Geological Survey led a full-fledged geological expedition which resulted in the first important geological book on the Grand Canyon, *The Tertiary History of the Grand Canyon District, with Atlas.*

1882: The tracks for the Atlantic and Pacific Railroad were laid. The railroad followed a route surveyed by General William J. Palmer in 1867–1868, passing near the San Francisco Peaks and Bill Williams Mountain. Railroad camps such as Flagstaff, Williams, and Peach Springs were established. By 1883, the stop at Peach Springs on the Hualapai Reservation was the closest the railroad came to the Grand Canyon, and tourists began to make the 20-mile journey to the Canyon fairly often.

1882–1883: Geologist Charles Doolittle Walcott traveled with Powell into the Grand Canyon. In order to take in its horses and equipment, this expedition enlarged the Nankoweap Trail, leading down into the eastern end of the Canyon along the route of an old Indian trail.

1883: The area of the present Hualapai Reservation was set aside, and this was confirmed by order of President Chester A. Arthur.

1883: "Captain" John Hance arrived at the Grand Canyon and became the first white resident. He was a memorable storyteller, tourist guide, trailbuilder, and miner. He built a log cabin at the head of the Old Hance Trail. The first tourists known to have visited John Hance at the Grand Canyon were Edward Everett Ayer and his family and friends.

1885: Hance hired Philip and William Hull, who had a sheep ranch south of the Canyon, as guides. They made a trip to the bottom of the Canyon, giving Mrs. Ayer the distinction of being the first white woman to make the descent on foot.

1886: Businessmen in Flagstaff began the campaign for a rail line by organizing the Flagstaff and Grand Canyon Railroad Company and running a survey, but financial backing could not be secured at that time.

1890: William Wallace Bass set up a camp on the South Rim near Havasupai Point, and completed a road to Ashfork.

1890–1891: Peter D. Berry, along with Ralph and Niles Cameron, widened Bright Angel Trail, which had been an old Havasupai Indian track, as far as Indian Garden.

1891: Louis D. Boucher, "The Hermit," came to the Grand Canyon. He rode a white mule with a bell around its neck. His home camp was at Dripping Springs. His Silver Bell Trail descended from the rim to Dripping Springs and then out around Columbus Point into Long (Boucher) Canyon. There he planted a splendid orchard and garden and grew grapes, oranges, figs, peaches, pomegranates and other fruits, and vegetables of every kind, including tomatoes, chilies, and cucumbers. He had 75 trees. This orchard was near the site of Boucher's copper mine, where tourists could stay in cabins.

1892–1893: Peter D. Berry built the four-mile Grandview Trail from Grandview Point down to his mine, the "Last Chance."

1893: Daniel L. Hogan located a claim for a gold mine a thousand feet below Maricopa Point. Since he was an orphan, he named it the "Orphan Mine." He and others built a trail down into that area from Horsethief Tank, which he had also constructed.

1893: The Grand Canyon was proclaimed a forest reserve by President Benjamin Harrison.

1894: Hance built the Red Canyon, or New Hance, Trail, when rockslides made the old trail unusable.

1894: A creek was named. Peter D. Berry and Ralph and Niles Cameron, along with James McClure, were traveling along the Tonto Platform between the Grandview Trail and the Bright Angel Trail. Ralph Cameron was ahead of the others. In a stream bed he found an old Meerschaum pipe. He picked it up, scratched a date about one hundred years previous on it, and put it where the others could not miss it. His companions fell for the joke, speculating on who might have been there so long before. The story was too good not to tell. The stream has been called Pipe Creek ever since.

1894: The citizens of Williams contributed $1000 to finance a survey for a railway.

1895: To finance a survey for a railway, Hance sold his ranch and trail to J. Wilber Thurber, who operated a stage line from Flagstaff. Hance continued to live at his ranch.

1896: The Bright Angel Hotel, an early tourist accommodation in Grand Canyon Village, was brought into service.

1896: BIA agent Henry P. Ewing was appointed to the Walapai Indian Agency, which supervised both tribes. He began to collect fees for grazing and timber-cutting on the reservation.

1897: Hance became the first postmaster on the rim of the Grand Canyon when the post office of Tourist, Arizona was established at Hance Ranch.

1897: The Santa Fe and Grand Canyon Railway Company was organized by Lombard, Goode and Company, to build a railroad and telegraph line from Williams to Grand Canyon. An act of Congress was required, granting right of way across the Grand Canyon Forest Reserve. The Grand Canyon was placed under the General Land Office of the Department of the Interior.

1898: Bright Angel Trail was extended down to the river.

1901: Peter D. Berry sold his Last Chance Mine to the Canyon Copper Company, an eastern consortium.

1901: The first scheduled train traveled from Williams to the Grand Canyon. The almost total lack of permanent surface water at the Grand Canyon was the most pressing problem in the development of the area. All water was hauled in railroad tank cars over distances of 60–120 miles.

1902: The first automobile known to make the trip to the Grand Canyon was a remarkable steam-driven automobile, a new Toledo eight-horse-power Locomobile. It chugged out of Flagstaff toward the Grand Canyon, but ran out of gas 18 miles from the Canyon. Pete Berry hauled gas from the railroad terminal to the machine, which was finally nursed up to the South Rim five days after it had left Flagstaff. The first automobiles to go to the North Rim were a Locomobile and a Thomas Flyer. They left Kanab in June 1909 and made the trip in three days. Gasoline had been cached in advance along the way.

1902: Ellsworth L. Kolb and Emery C. Kolb came to the Grand Canyon. The Kolb brothers became nationally known for their boat trip down the Colorado River in 1911–1912, which was the first to be recorded on motion picture film. Emery gave lectures on the river trips and the Canyon for sixty years. He died in 1976, at age 95, and is buried beside his wife and brother in Pioneer Cemetery at Grand Canyon.

1902: Francois Emile Matthes began the first topographic map of the Grand Canyon. He began his map for the U.S. Geological Survey on the South Rim, establishing bench marks and using triangulation, leveling, and plane-table methods to establish the position and levation of points which could be seen from the rim. During scorching days on the Hance Trail, the rocks became so hot that the men had to shift continually from one foot to the other to avoid burning. Matthes named Krishna Shrine, Solomon Temple, Wotan's Throne, and Walhalla Plateau.

1903: Theodore Roosevelt visited the Grand Canyon. He was deeply moved by the beauty of the Canyon, and remarked that it was "to me the most impressive piece of scenery I have ever looked at."

1903: Arthur R. Sanger, John A. King, and their boatman, E. B. "Hum" Woolley (all of whom were apparently miners) left Lees Ferry in August for a trek in their 18-foot oaken boat. By the end of October, they had reached Yuma.

1903: The Supai Post Office opened. This required the mail carrier to travel over a long, rough trail to the Havasupai Indian community in its alcove of the Grand Canyon.

1905: A first-class hotel, El Tovar, was opened. Combining the architectural flavors of a Swiss chateau and a castle on the Rhine, it was made of native boulders and Douglas fir logs. The building cost $250,000 to construct. It was named El Tovar in honor of the Spanish explorer who had visited the Hopi towns (but not the Grand Canyon) in 1540. A replica of an Indian pueblo, called the Hopi House, was constructed nearby. John G. Verkamp had been running the first curio stand in a tent of the Bright Angel Hotel. In 1905, he built a curio store east of the Hopi House which still exists.

1906: Martin Buggeln, former manager of the Bright Angel Hotel, bought Hance Ranch and built a white, 17-room frame hotel beside the old log dining room.

1906: The Grand Canyon Game Preserve was set aside, and soon afterwards James T. "Uncle Jim" Owens was appointed warden by the Forest Service.

1907: The bottom dropped out of the copper market. New methods had been developed for processing low-grade ore, and the high-grade ore of the Last Chance Mine was no longer worth hauling out of the canyon.

1907: A cable crossing the river was installed at the mouth of Bright Angel Creek.

1908: Theodore Roosevelt declared portions of the Grand Canyon a National Monument.

1908: William Wallace Bass installed a cableway across the river at Bass Crossing, with a cage big enough to carry a burro. It was soon enlarged to permit a mule or horse to be sent across. Later, he built another cableway three river miles below, near the mouth of Hakatai Canyon. The cables remained in place until 1968, when they were removed as a hazard to aircraft.

1909: The first sportsman's river trip was made by Julius F. Stone, an Ohio manufacturer. Companions were Seymour S. Deubendorff and Nathaniel Galloway, who designed a boat that was decked-over, except for a cockpit in which a single oarsman sat. The trip from Green River, Wyoming, to Needles was made in only 10 weeks.

1910: The flood of 1910 swept away most of the homes, as well as the school, of the Havasupai Indian community. The first Master Plan for Grand Canyon was written by the U.S. Forest Service, who managed the Grand Canyon untill 1919.

1914: Hermits Rest, a stone-and-log building where weary travelers could find refreshment, was built. The architect was Mary Colter.

1915: Neil M. Judd was the first professional archaeologist sent to investigate the Grand Canyon. The Bureau of American Ethnology hailed the proclamation of Grand Canyon National Monument as a means of protecting "innumerable antiquities, including cliff-dwellings, pueblos, dwelling sites, and burial places."

1916: The National Park Service was created, "To conserve the scenery and the natural and historic objects and the wildlife therein and to provide for the enjoyment of the same in such manner and by such means as will leave them unimpaired for the enjoyment of future generations."

1918: A monument to John Wesley Powell and the men of his two Colorado River expeditions was dedicated (it was built in 1916). The memorial is a truncated stone pyramid with a bronze plaque.

1919: President Woodrow Wilson signed the bill that created Grand Canyon National Park.

1919: The Hualapais elected a tribal council. They were encouraged by their agents to develop the extensive grazing lands in their reservation on the Grand Canyon's southern margin by building fences, charging grazing fees, and starting a herd of their own. They were troubled by the Santa Fe Railroad's claim to half those lands.

1919–1939: The National Park Service saw a clear need for many kinds of buildings as well as more roads. As soon as funds were available, construction began on administration buildings, residences, warehouses, a mess hall, a stable/garage, and a blacksmith shop. Many additional roads and buildings were built and improved during this period of intense construction.

1920: The Grand Canyon National Park was formally dedicated on April 30 in ceremonies at the Powell Memorial. The first director of the National Park Service, Stephen Tyng Mather, payed for many of the badly needed improvements in the early parks out of his own pocket. His memorial stands at Mather Point on the South Rim.

1926: Automobiles overtook the railroad as the most popular way to travel to the Canyon.

1926: A "recycling" plant for reclaiming wastewater, which could be used for non-potable purposes, began operating. It was designed by M.R. Tillotson and continues to be regarded as an excellent example, far ahead of its time, of effective conservation of a precious resource.

1926: A considerable number of Havasupais found employment in Grand Canyon Village, both with concessionaire Fred Harvey and the National Park Service, which recognized their special status within the park. Many Indians lived in a camp near Grand Canyon Village. But without medical attention, proper housing, or adequate water, the camp was a rural slum. In the mid-1930s, the National Park Service provided new cabins, and the Bureau of Indian Affairs made arrangements with the resident physician to give medical care. The Havasupai children began to attend the Grand Canyon School.

1928: With the erection of a rigid suspension bridge to replace the old swinging bridge, the cross-canyon Kaibab Trail was finished to "high standard of pack animal construction." The eight cables were so heavy that 42 Havasupai Indians were hired to station themselves at intervals, lift the cable to their shoulders, and proceed down the trail like a gigantic centipede.

1928: A fine observation station/museum was erected at Yavapai Point through a grant by the Laura Spelman Rockefeller Foundation. The museum had fixed binoculars pointed at important locations in the Canyon.

1928: The Union Pacific Railroad installed a powerhouse and pumping plant on Bright Angel Creek near Roaring Springs, bringing a dependable supply of water to the North Rim. That same year, the U.S. Government took over Bright Angel Trail.

1929: A new Park Headquarters was built in the new village area south of the railroad tracks.

1929: Airplane service first became available across the Grand Canyon.

1929: Marble Canyon Bridge was dedicated near Lees Ferry, making one- or two-day vehicle travel possible between the North and South Rims.

1930: Hermit Camp was abandoned when the opening of the Bright Angel Trail to free travel and the construction of the new South Kaibab Trail and Phantom Ranch made it redundant.

1931: The scarcity of surface water and increasing visitation necessitated the building of a pipeline from the waters of Garden Creek at Indian Garden to the South Rim.

1932: A new Grand Canyon National Monument was proclaimed by President Herbert C. Hoover. Toroweap was an area of over 300 square miles adjoining the national park on the west, and extending 40 miles along the Colorado River.

1932: The Desert View Watchtower, designed by the inimitable Mary Colter, was erected at the end of Desert View or East Rim Drive.

1935–1936: Hoover Dam was completed, and Lake Mead National Recreation Area was established.

1936: Construction began on the second North Rim Lodge to replace the original building which was destroyed by fire.

1937: A good approach road from the east, through Cameron and Desert View, was paved. This gave the South Rim two entrances. There were 300,000 visitors to the Grand Canyon during this year, and a Ford Tri-motor airplane flew the Canyon on a regular basis.

1938: The approach road from Kanab, Utah was completely paved. The Navajo or Marble Canyon Bridge was also paved, reducing the distance from South Rim to North Rim to its present 215 road miles.

1944: During this war year, only 65,000 visitors came, and many of these were servicemen on trips arranged for their units.

1948: The states of the Upper Colorado River Basin recommended the Colorado River Storage Project, including dams in Glen Canyon and Echo Park. Conservationists kept Echo Park Dam out of the bill, protecting Dinosaur National Monument. But, when the gates closed in 1964, Glen

Canyon Dam flooded a larger area, including many historic and prehistoric sites. The days of the spring flood and the untamed river were over.

1951: The Geological Survey discovered that the Orphan Mine lode was rich in uranium. The mine was put into production by the Golden Crown Mining Company three years later. With the advent of the Atomic Age, the Orphan became the only active mine in Grand Canyon National Park. It passed into NPS hands in 1987.

1955: Construction began on new facilities at the South Rim as part of the National Park Service Mission 66 program.

1956: There were 1 million visitors to the park, and reservations were required.

1956: One of commercial aviation's worst disasters took place. Near noon on a reasonably clear day in June, two airliners on eastward flights from Los Angeles collided over the Canyon and fell into the gorge near the river, killing all 128 people aboard. This collision resulted in the establishment of a national air traffic control system.

1960: The largest fire in Grand Canyon history, the Saddle Mountain Blaze, took place. It destroyed about 9,000 acres, mostly in the Kaibab National Forest but including 300 acres of park land.

1964: Glen Canyon Dam began electrical generation.

1964: 900 people ran the Colorado River.

1969: There were over 2 million visitors, yet the Vietnam crisis caused the government to cut appropriations for staff and facilities.

1970: Construction was completed on a pipeline that ran from Roaring Springs below the North Rim all the way down Bright Angel Canyon, across the river on a new suspension bridge, and up to the pumping station at Indian Garden by gravity flow.

1970: Nearly 10,000 people ran the Colorado River.

1972: Visitation reached 2,700,000, but declined in the next two years due to fuel shortage and rising costs brought about by the Middle East conflict.

1974: An epoch on the Colorado River ended when Emery Kolb made his last trip in Grand Canyon, at the age of 93, as a passenger on Dock Marston's boat. His journey took him from the Little Colorado River to Crystal Rapid.

1975: The Historic District was established, and Hopi House was included in the district. The Grand Canyon Enlargement Act added Marble Canyon, NM, and Grand Canyon, NM, to Grand Canyon National Park.

1976: Visitation to the Grand Canyon passed 3 million.

1979: Grand Canyon National Park was designated a World Heritage Site.

1980–1981: After 17 years, Lake Powell filled.

1980–1981: Fund for Animals removed feral burros from the Grand Canyon.

1983: A record post-dam flood scoured the Canyon. Some rapids bacame impossible, stranding river trip passengers temporarily.

1989: Rail passenger service to the South Rim of the Grand Canyon was restored by owners of the new Grand Canyon Railway.

1992: The Grand Canyon Protection Act required operation of the Glen Canyon Dam to mitigate adverse impacts caused by widely fluctuating water levels in short periods on the Colorado River through Grand Canyon National Park.

1994: Grand Canyon celebrated its 75th anniversary as a national park.

1995: The General Management Plan for Grand Canyon was released with the goals of significantly reducing the use of automobiles and improving the visitor experience in Grand Canyon National Park.

1996: Six California condors were released at Vermilion Cliffs as part of a reintroduction program for this endangered species.

1997: Secretary of the Interior Bruce Babbitt called for the removal of 80 percent of all automobiles from Grand Canyon National Park.

1999: The Canyon Forest Village plan was approved by Coconino County Planning & Zoning Commission. The village will be a complex of stores, restaurants, lodging, and employee housing located between Tusayan and the South Entrance to the park.

2000: To meet the goals of the General Management Plan, the first phase of a new transportation plan for Grand Canyon National Park was implemented. The plan provides for year-round shuttle service on the South Rim, and the development of a new transportation center near Mather Point on the South Rim.

Grand Canyon National Park is challenged by increasing visitation. To protect and preserve the wild and unimpaired nature of the Grand Canyon for the future and to provide educational materials for visitors, several nonprofit organizations have been established. The Grand Canyon Association and the Grand Canyon National Park Foundation work in partnership with the National Park Service and each other to provide educational materials and opportunities for visitors to contribute to the Grand Canyon's preservation. The Grand Canyon Trust (GCT) is a conservation organization dedicated to protecting the resources and wildlands of the Colorado Plateau, including Grand Canyon National Park. In addition, the NPS operates an Environmental Education Program at the Grand Canyon that provides school, group, and individual learning experiences in the park. Here's more information about each organization, including how you can help in the effort to support Grand Canyon National Park for future generations.

The Grand Canyon Association (GCA) is a nonprofit educational organization founded in 1932 to aid educational, historical, and scientific programs for the benefit of Grand Canyon National Park and its visitors. Among other activities, the GCA:

⇨ Operates bookstores in visitor centers throughout the park, with proceeds going to support park programs;

⇨ Founded the Grand Canyon Field Institute in 1993, which offers educational courses for all ages that enhance visitor understanding and enjoyment of the park through firsthand experience;

⇨ Publishes trail guides as well as more than two million pieces of free informational literature for park visitors each year;

⇨ Funds a variety of exhibits throughout the park;

⇨ Administers grants and gifts received for designated projects in the Grand Canyon;

⇨ Helps support wildlife surveys and other important research;

⇨ Provides continued support to Grand Canyon's research library through purchase of materials and employment of staff;

⇨ Organizes curriculum workshops for teachers, and teaches children about Grand Canyon geology, ecology, and history.

To join the association, or for more information, call (800) 858-2808 or (520) 638-2481. You can write them at P.O. Box 399, Grand Canyon, Arizona 86023, or visit their website at www.grandcanyon.org. You can find a membership application on page 179.

The Grand Canyon National Park Foundation is a nonprofit organization incorporated in 1995. It operates under an agreement with the National Park Service, with the goal of helping to preserve, protect, and enhance Grand Canyon National Park and to enrich each visitor's experience. The Foundation receives no federal funding and is not a membership organization. The park can no longer depend on federal appropriations, which are lagging behind the park's growing needs. To help, the Foundation funds important projects and programs in support of the park, including exhibits, wildlife restoration projects, and interpretive programs. Its funds come from the support of private citizens, foundations, and corporations. To make a donation to the Grand Canyon National Park Foundation, call them at (520) 774-1760, fax them at (520) 774-1240, write them at 823 N. San Francisco, Suite A, Flagstaff, AZ 86001, or visit them online at www.grandcanyonfoundation.org. You can find a Foundation donor form on page 182.

The Grand Canyon Trust (GCT) is a national, nonprofit conservation organization founded in 1985, dedicated to the preservation and protection of the spectacular wildlands and resources of the Colorado Plateau. Some of their conservation projects include:

⇨ Helping to preserve clean air for the Canyon by working to get air pollution controls installed at the Navajo Power Plant at the eastern end of the park;

⇨ Helping to preserve healthy forests by launching the Grand Canyon Forests Partnership, an ambitious project to restore 100,000 acres of ponderosa pine forests;

⇨ Restoring Colorado River habitat by helping to engineer the 1996 flood flow plan to restore beaches in the Grand Canyon;

⇨ Working to help manage the Glen Canyon Dam to benefit downstream natural resources;

⇨ Working to preserve the natural quiet and solitude of the Canyon by controlling excessive air tours over the Grand Canyon.

To join the Grand Canyon Trust, call them at (888) GCT-5550 or (520) 774-7488, write them at 2601 N. Fort Valley Rd., Flagstaff, Arizona 86001, or visit their website at www.grandcanyontrust.org. You can find a GCT membership form on page 181.

NPS Environmental Education Programs. The NPS operates, and is always in the process of developing, a variety of programs to help individuals, schools, and community groups learn more about the park and the need to protect park resources. These programs include:

⇨ On-site, educational field trips;

⇨ School curriculum for teachers, and teacher-training workshops;

⇨ Area field trips;

⇨ An on-site environmental education center;

⇨ Environmental Youth Corps opportunities;

⇨ "Family Backpacks," available at the South Rim Visitor Center;

⇨ Interpretive programs in schools;

⇨ Educational materials for international visitors;

⇨ Native American community education programs.

For more information about these and other educational opportunities at the Grand Canyon, call the Education Office at (520) 638-7762.

Recycling. Grand Canyon National Park has instituted a comprehensive and successful park-wide recycling program for aluminum, glass, and plastic products. Park visitors are encouraged to deposit aluminum cans and glass in special receptacles located in all developed areas and campgrounds. Grand Canyon National Park Lodges has also implemented a comprehensive recycling program throughout the park, which recycles newspapers, plastic, glass, and aluminum from all guest accommodations on a daily basis.

THINGS TO DO WITH KIDS

Interactive Reading/Exploring. The Grand Canyon Association (GCA) has a great "kid's pack," filled with reading and comic books for kids who want to know more about the Grand Canyon. Stop by one of the GCA bookstores while you're in the park to find other selections for kids, including: *Exploring the Grand Canyon: Adventures of Yesterday and Today* by Lynne Foster; the charming *Brighty of the Grand Canyon* by Marguerite Henry; the traditional Hopi tale of *Coyote & Little Turtle, Creatures of the Desert World* by the National Geographic Society; and the vividly illustrated *101 Questions about Desert Life* by Alice Jablonsky. GCA bookstores are located throughout the park, or call (800) 858-2808 to order books or receive a publications catalog.

Take a River-Rafting Trip. For an experience your kids will always remember, take them on a smooth-water (leisurely day of floating) or white-water (more exciting and active experience) rafting trip down the Colorado River. Most trips are offered spring through fall. Call (800) 528-6154 or (520) 645-3279. You can also visit the South Rim Visitor Center for more information on the smooth-water trip. Refer to pages 191–192 for a list of white-water rafting outfitters.

Take a Hike or Walk with a Ranger. It's an easy hike from Yavapai Observation Station or the visitor center to Maricopa Point. You can try a self-guided nature trail, or take a walk with a park ranger (see page 80). Popular topics include searching for fossils on South Kaibab Trail, and sunset nature hikes. Be sure to check *The Guide* newspaper for current schedules and locations.

Visit the Tusayan Indian Ruin and Museum. Explore the secrets left behind by the ancestral Pueblo people who lived in the Grand Canyon 800 years ago. Visit the museum to discover clues—pottery, drawings on rocks, split-twig figurines—that they left behind about how they lived.

Become a Junior Ranger. This popular program, designed for kids from 4 to 14, helps young visitors learn about the care and protection of park resources by completing a list of fun activities. Pick up a copy of *Junior Ranger* at any visitor or information center in the park, and your kids will be on their way to earning a Junior Ranger certificate.

Visit the Mule Corral. Even though you may not be old enough to ride a mule into the Canyon, it's great fun just to hang out in the morning at the mule corrals and watch the mule riders getting ready for the trip. Just remember to stay outside the corral.

Ride a Horse-Drawn Wagon into Kaibab National Forest. At twilight, you can catch a ride in a real horse-drawn wagon. Rides head out from Moqui Lodge. For reservations and information call (520) 638-2891, or ask at lodging desks throughout the park.

Enjoy a Western-Style Cookout. You can cook your own meal the way the pioneers did, over an open campfire. Cookouts are offered daily, from May to the first snow, from Moqui Lodge. A great western experience for the whole family. Call (520) 638-2891 for reservations and information.

Campfire Programs. Come to a family campfire program to hear tales about prospectors and Native Americans, as well as stories about burros and bighorns. Check *The Guide*, or at any visitor center, for program times and locations.

Kid Discounts. Kids 16 years and under ride free on any Canyon bus tour when accompanied by an adult family member. Special reduced-price menus for kids are available in most restaurants. Call Grand Canyon National Park Lodges at (520) 638-2631, or stop at lodging desks.

BACKCOUNTRY PERMITS REQUEST FORM

BACKCOUNTRY PERMIT REQUEST FORM
Backcountry Office, Grand Canyon National Park
PO Box 129, Grand Canyon, AZ 86023

FAX (520)638-2125

Name: _____ Home Phone: _____

Address: _____ Work Phone: _____

City: _____ State: _____ Zip: _____

Country: _____ Organization: _____

# of People: _____ # of Equines: _____ Vehicle #1 State: _____ Lic. Plate: _____ Vehicle #2 State: _____ Lic. Plate: _____

First Choice:

	Date	Use Area or Campsite
1	_____	_____
2	_____	_____
3	_____	_____
4	_____	_____
5	_____	_____
6	_____	_____

Second Choice:

	Date	Use Area or Campsite
1	_____	_____
2	_____	_____
3	_____	_____
4	_____	_____
5	_____	_____
6	_____	_____

Third Choice:

	Date	Use Area or Campsite
1	_____	_____
2	_____	_____
3	_____	_____
4	_____	_____
5	_____	_____
6	_____	_____

WILLING TO ACCEPT VARIATIONS: ☐ STARTDATE (BETWEEN _____ AND _____) ☐ CAMPSITES ☐ TRIP LENGTH (___ MAXIMUM) (AFFECTS COST)

Method of Payment: ☐ VISA ☐ MasterCard ☐ Discover

Credit Card Number:

Exp. Date: _____ Cardholder: _____

Total Authorized Permit Cost $ _____

(Charge is $10 plus $5 per person per night.)

(Hikers also will be responsible for paying park entrance fees upon arrival.)

Signature: _____ Date: _____

☐ In place of the $10 above, enroll me in the Frequent Hiker Program for $25 for a year. Waives the initial $10 permit fee for each permit obtained by the member trip leader.

176

BACKCOUNTRY PERMITS: INFORMATION, DEADLINES, AND CONSTRAINTS

Canyon hikers are fully responsible for knowing and obeying all regulations. Backpackers are responsible for their own safety and for costs should a rescue be initiated. Please research carefully as you plan for a safe trip. Trail guides and maps may be purchased at www.thecanyon.com/gca.

Currently, costs include a $10 basic permit-processing fee plus a $5 per person per night impact fee. Frequent users may wish to purchase a 1-year Frequent Hiker membership for $25. This membership waives the $10 basic permit-processing fee for each permit obtained by the member trip leader. The membership is valid for 1 year from the date of purchase. **All fees paid to to the Backcountry Information Center are NON-REFUNDABLE!** If a cancellation is processed by the Backcountry Information Center at least 3 days before a start-date, a 1-year office credit will be issued for the impact fee (the $10 permit processing fee will be forfeited). Denied requests do not incur a charge.

Permit requests are not accepted by telephone. Requests can be faxed to (520) 638-2125. Permit requests are considered when postmarked or faxed no earlier than the first of the month 4 months before a start date. For example, requests postmarked on or after May 1, 2000 can ask for start dates through September 30, 2000. It is common for the Backcountry Information Center to receive 100 to 400 letters and faxes per day for the first 3 weeks that a month opens: please allow 3 to 6 weeks for your request to be processed. Due to the volume of requests, the Backcountry Information Center will not check the status of requests which have not been processed. When sending in a permit request, the preferred method of payment is by credit card (VISA, MasterCard, or DISCOVER only). Please be sure to indicate the maximum amount you authorize the Backcountry Information Center to charge so your longest alternative can be considered.

While the validity of a request is determined by the date sent (postmark), requests are processed by the Backcountry Information Center in the order of the date received. Should the Backcountry Information Center begin accepting requests directly through the Internet (www.thecanyon.com/nps), this process will change to allow those without access to the Internet a chance to compete. Until that time, written requests received on the same day are processed randomly.

Duplicate requests will result in duplicate, non-refundable charges! Requests can be faxed or mailed to the address listed at the top of the permit request form. Overnight mail can be sent to the following address: Backcountry Information Center, 1 Village Loop Road, Grand Canyon, AZ 86023.

In-person requests are also considered up to 4 months in advance as stated above. Walk-in requests are limited to 3 requests per person and are processed immediately. Additional written requests are considered to be hand-delivered mail and will be processed randomly with all mail received that day. The South Rim Backcountry Information Center is open 8 a.m. to 12 noon and 1 p.m. to 5 p.m. MST. Arizona does not observe Daylight Savings Time.

Additional written information may be obtained by writing to the Backcountry Information Center or calling (520) 638-7888. A voice-mail system will handle your call, and recorded messages are available to answer most questions. If you wish to speak to Backcountry Information Center Personnel, you can call direct at (520) 638-7875. Phones are answered 1 p.m. to 5 p.m. MST, Monday through Friday, except federal holidays. Please realize this is an extremely busy phone line, and you may need to try several times before getting through.

The North Rim Backcountry Information Center is open from 8 a.m. to 12 noon and from 1 p.m. to 5 p.m. from approximately mid-May through late October. Due to severe weather, the North Rim is closed at other times. Access is subject to road closures beyond the control of Grand Canyon National Park.

GRAND CANYON ASSOCIATION MEMBERSHIP FORM

Yes, I want to support education and research
at Grand Canyon National Park by becoming a
member of Grand Canyon Association.

Name_____

Name on second *Family* card _____

Address _____

City _____State_____Zip _____

Phone (day) _____

Phone (eve.) _____
    Please send me updates on GCA activities via
email; my address is _____

ENCLOSED ARE MY ANNUAL DUES OF:
    Individual $35   Guarantor $500
    Family $50   Grand Circle $1,000
    Contributor $100   Canyon Society $2,500
    Sponsor $250   Donation $_____

Please do not send me any premiums. I want
my membership to be 100% tax-deductible. I understand that I will receive *Canyon Views*, as well as
discounts on merchandise and selected Grand
Canyon Field Institute courses.

PAYMENT:
For *Contributor* and above only:
    Please bill me in installments
        monthly   quarterly   semiannually
    Enclosed is my first installment of $ _____

Enclosed is my check for $ _____
    Charge my *(check one):*
        American Express   Visa   MasterCard

Acct. # _____ Expires_____

Signature _____

    Please do *not* make my name available to other
non-profit organizations.

*For more information or to enroll by phone call (800)
858-2808. Visit our web site at www.grandcanyon.org.*

GRAND CANYON TRUST

Grand Canyon Trust is a national, non-profit conservation organization dedicated to protecting and restoring the Grand Canyon region.
Founded in 1985, we have an impressive track record of success. The
Grand Canyon Trust is headquartered in Flagstaff, Arizona with field
offices in Moab and St. George, Utah.

*"The Grand Canyon Trust is one of the most effective conservation
organizations I know. Through their work on some of the West's thorniest
natural resource issues, they have shown an unequaled ability to get the
job done."*

—**Stewart L. Udall**

The Grand Canyon Trust works to preserve the slick rock canyons,
spectacular landscapes, flowing rivers, and diversity of nature in the
Grand Canyon and across the Colorado Plateau through these and
other key projects:

⇨ Clean air for the Canyon. Air pollution controls are now installed
at the Navajo power plant at the eastern end of the park, thanks
to the Trust's work. Now we are working to clean up the Mohave
Power Plant to the west.

⇨ Healthy forests. We have launched the Grand Canyon Forests
Partnership, an ambitious project to restore 100,000 acres of
ponderosa pine forests.

⇨ Restored Colorado River habitat. We helped engineer the March
1996 flood flow to restore beaches in the Grand Canyon and
now work to manage Glen Canyon Dam to benefit downstream
natural resources.

⇨ Preserve natural quiet and solitude. We are fighting to control
over 100,000 sightseeing air tours over the Grand Canyon *each
year* and we are working for Congressional action to restrict noisy
flights in all our national parks.

**Your contribution will help protect and restore
the Grand Canyon for the next millennium.**

GRAND CANYON TRUST

SIGN ME UP! I want to conserve the Grand Canyon and the canyon country of the Colorado Plateau as a member of the Grand Canyon Trust. *Simply fill out the form below.*

Name _____

Address _____

City/State/Zip _____

Phone _____ Email _____

Choose a membership option:

❑ Annual . . . .$35   ❑ Defender $50

❑ Protector . . . . . .$100   ❑ Guardian $250

❑ Patron . . . .$500   ❑ John Wesley Powell Society $1000

❑ Limited Income $15

❑ Enclosed is my check or money order

❑ Please charge my Visa/Mastercard

❑ Please charge my American Express

Account # _____ Exp Date _____

Signature _____

Please make checks payable to:

**Grand Canyon Trust
P.O. Box 1236
Flagstaff, AZ 86002**

Toll Free (888) GCT-5550
501 (c) 3 tax deductible

FORMS

GRAND CANYON NATIONAL PARK FOUNDATION DONOR FORM

See page 172 for information about the Grand Canyon National Park Foundation.

Be a Part of Something Grand! We pledge to employ the same stewardship values in the use of your generous contribution as we do in protecting Grand Canyon National Park. Your gift in any amount *does* make a difference.

Yes! I'd like to help with my gift of:

☐ $25   ☐ $50   ☐ $100   ☐ $1,000   ☐ $ other _____

Name _____

Address _____

City _____

State _____

Zip _____

Phone _____

☐ Enclosed is my check payable to:
   Grand Canyon National Park Foundation at NPF

☐ Charge my gift to   ☐ MC ☐ VISA

Name as it appears on card _____

Card number _____

Expiration date _____

Signature _____

Please remove or photocopy this form and send it with your donation to:

The Grand Canyon National Park Foundation
823 N. San Francisco, Suite A
Flagstaff, AZ 86001
(520) 774-1760

Big Jim

A member of the Havasupai Indian tribe, "Big Jim" had the longest association with the Grand Canyon's pioneer era. For generations, maybe centuries, Big Jim's family (Vesna) held traditional rights to the acres surrounding the springs at Indian Garden, north of today's Grand Canyon Village and 3,000 vertical feet below the South Rim. Big Jim was born at these springs in the 1850s. Many Havasupai would spend summers away from the tribe's primary village in Havasu Canyon, enjoying the solitude of more remote areas with perennial springs. During the summers, Big Jim and his family would sleep in wickiups beside the springs, set wildfires to condition the soil, irrigate a small plot of peach trees and vegetables, and fill stacked-stone bins in nearby cliffs with emergency food supplies. Each autumn his family would climb up to the rim on a centuries-old foot-path along natural breaks in the stone caused by the Bright Angel Fault, returning to their village in Havasu Canyon.

For nine decades, Big Jim interacted with the first white pioneers who came and eventually settled at the South Rim. He helped early set-tlers find their way in the area, moving between his summer home at Indian Garden and several winter homes on the rim. By the 1920s, he had become a headman among his people and a local celebrity among residents of Grand Canyon Village. A tall, stately man, he would often come to the village wearing a frock coat, top hat, and an official decoration given to him by King Albert of Belgium (a Canyon visitor). Big Jim lived near the south central rim of the Grand Canyon until the late 1940s.

John Wesley Powell

Like John Muir, Major John Wesley Powell was one of a distinctive group of self-taught nineteenth-century Renaissance men who trav-eled throughout the American West and wrote extensively about the experience. In 1869, he led the first organized expedition down 1,000 miles of the Colorado River, going through the Grand Canyon. It was a truly remarkable feat, accomplished in four small wooden boats and on meager rations. This was followed by a series of expeditions and the Powell Survey (1870–1874), during which he surveyed and mapped the Colorado River and its tributaries, naming virtually all the rapids and other features encountered along the river as it winds through the Canyon. He is credited with giving the name "Bright Angel" to the area, and with helping to build the Nankoweap Trail on the North Rim. Following his surveying work, this one-armed Civil

War veteran founded the U.S. Geological Survey and the U.S. Bureau of American Ethnology. He was an early and ardent advocate of the wise use of water in the West, and of Native American rights.

Captain John Hance

Captain John Hance was perhaps the Grand Canyon's most colorful resident and premier storyteller. He is said to have been the first white settler in the Canyon, first visiting the South Rim before 1881 and staying until his death in 1919. Hance built a guest ranch in 1883 (Hance Ranch) and improved an old Havasupai trail along Hance Creek, three miles east of Grandview Point, to access his mining claims in the Canyon. But after leading a prominent couple down into the Canyon in 1884, he decided tourism would be a better source of income. In 1886 he built a cabin at the head of the trail and began to run advertisements inviting tourists to Hance Ranch. His tourist accomodations were rustic and had few comforts, but the expert guide and lifelong bachelor only charged one dollar for a night's lodging, including dinner. He also rented complete camping outfits, including pack and saddle horses, trail clothing, and supplies. When a landslide covered the trail in 1894, Hance built a better one, known today as the New Hance Trail, which runs down Red Canyon east of his ranch. He became one of the Canyon's most flamboyant storytellers, entertaining his guests with "whoppers" on a regular basis. He typically sported a full goatee and mustache, and was seldom seen without a hat. He dressed in buckskins, or in the turn-of-the-century garb of prospectors. This polite and gentle man had an uncanny ability to hoodwink listeners with his legendary storytelling. Many of his tall tales are retold today by park rangers in campfire programs.

Mary Elizabeth Jane Colter

Mary Elizabeth Jane Colter was one of the rare women in the late 1800s who attended architectural school, worked as an architectural apprentice, and became a professional architect. In 1902, she was offered a job as a designer for the Fred Harvey Company, which was developing tourist properties along the South Rim of the Grand Canyon. This relationship was to last forty-six years, resulting in seven historic South Rim structures and the only remaining Inner Canyon resort. Colter was fascinated by Southwestern Native American cultures and heritage, an interest that was reflected in such projects as the Watchtower at Desert View and the Hopi House. Her remarkable ability to highlight and reflect the natural beauty of the surrounding parklands is seen in such projects as Hermit's Rest, Lookout Studio, Bright Angel Lodge, and Phantom Ranch. She also designed the interior of the El Tovar Hotel. At Phantom Ranch, look for the four cabins of mostly native stone and the north half of the lodge dining room to get a sense of her original design for this project, which cost $20,000 to build. Colter's buildings leave behind a rich architectural vernacular for the Grand Canyon.

William Owen "Buckey" O'Neill

A restless adventurer, newspaper owner, and local politician, "Buckey" O'Neill came to the South Rim area in the 1890s, looking for mining claims. When he discovered a long belt of copper deposits running south towards Williams, O'Neill decided that a railroad should be built from Williams to the South Rim, where he envisioned an area devoted to tourist facilities. It was because of O'Neill's tireless lobbying efforts, both locally and nationally, that the Santa Fe and Grand Canyon Railway was first formed in 1897, with "General" Buckey O'Neill and others as directors. In 1901, after the company suffered financing woes, the Santa Fe Pacific Railroad bought the nearly completed railroad and finished laying tracks under the name of the Grand Canyon Railway.

And what happened to the man who was largely responsible for bringing trains to the Grand Canyon? In 1898, O'Neill became mayor of Prescott, Arizona, and quickly volunteered to serve in the Spanish-American War with Teddy Roosevelt and the Rough Riders. He was killed in action just before the charge up San Juan Hill. Today, you can ride the Grand Canyon Railway to the South Rim, and stay in the Buckey O'Neill cabin at the Bright Angel Lodge.

The Kolb Brothers (Ellsworth and Emery)

In 1902 the two Kolb brothers bought out a Williams photography studio, and set up shop on the South Rim of Grand Canyon to take photographs of the ever-increasing flow of tourists. Their first studio was a dirt-floor tent next to Ralph Cameron's hotel. They used a shallow mine shaft as a darkroom, and developed prints with murky water from cattle ponds far from the site. In 1904 they upgraded to a small frame studio on Cameron's mining claim at the Bright Angel Trailhead. With additions in 1915 and 1925, the Kolb Brothers' Lookout Studio today stands as one of the oldest buildings in Grand Canyon National Park. In 1905, Emery married, and in 1908, his daughter was the first European-American child delivered (and for

years the only European-American child to live) at the Grand
Canyon. In the winter of 1911–1912, the brothers made history by
filming the first motion picture of a river run, which they showed at
their studio and on numerous national lecture tours. The Kolb brothers earned a reputation as great photographers, expert guides, and
geographers. Although Ellsworth eventually moved to Los Angeles,
Emery stayed at the Grand Canyon for 73 years, until his death in
1976 at the age of 93. His was the longest recorded year-round resi-
dency at the Canyon. He left behind tens of thousands of photographs and several hundred pieces of camera equipment that tell a
fascinating story of the Grand Canyon experience.

GRAND CANYON COMMERCIAL BACKPACKERS, DAY HIKERS, BICYCLISTS

COMPANY	CONTACT	ACTIVITY	PHONE
Adventure Travel West Inc. PO Box 121 Idledale, CO 80453	Susanne Lorenz	Day Hiking	(303) 697-6688
Adventures in Good Company 5506 Trading Post Trail S. Afton, MN 55001	Marian Marbury	Backpacking	(651) 998-0120
Allibert Route de Grenoble, 38530 Chapareillan, FRANCE	Michel Vibert	Day Hiking	
Arizona Scenic Biking Co. 131 E. Wagon Wheel Phoenix, AZ 85020	Arthur Gordon	Bicycling	(602) 905-2453
Backroads 801 Cedar St. Berkeley, CA 94710	Cynthia Audet	Bicycling	(510) 527-1555
Canyon Dreams 119 Oneida Flagstaff, AZ 86001	Jim Justham	Backpacking Day Hiking	(520) 525-9434
Canyon Rim Adventures PO Box 304 Kanab, UT 84741	Trent Keller	Bicycling Day Hiking	(800) 897-9633
City of Flagstaff Parks & Rec. 211 W. Aspen Flagstaff, AZ 86001	Johnathon Koehn	Backpacking	(520) 779-7685
Colorado Outward Bound School PO Box M Moab, UT 84532	Jimbo Buikerood	Backpacking	(435) 259-4209
Cycle America PO Box 485 Cannon Falls, MN 55009	Andy Hill	Bicycling	(507) 263-2665
Discovery Treks 4025 Lake Mary Rd. #9 Flagstaff, AZ 86001	Robert Fliegel	Day Hiking	(520) 779-1089

Discovery Treks 8135 Fran Dr. Flagstaff, AZ 86004	Robert Fliegel	Backpacking	(888) 256-8731
Grand Canyon Day Hikes 427 Marina St. Prescott, AZ 86303	Romy Anne Murphy	Day Hiking	(520) 778-7566
Grand Canyon Outdoor Center, Inc. PO Box 3493 Flagstaff, AZ 86003	Jeni Wiskofske	Day Hiking	(520) 774-3377
Grand Canyon Trail Guides PO Box 3293 Grand Canyon, AZ 86023	Bill Vercammem	Backpacking	(820) 638-0160
Grand Canyon Trail Guides PO Box 87 Grand Canyon, AZ 86023	Bill Vercammen	Day Hiking	(520) 638-3194
High Sonoran Adventures 10628 N. 97 St. Scottsdale, AZ 85260	Denny Carr	Day Hiking Bicycling	(602) 614-3331
Indiana University 900 E. Seventh St. Bloomington, IN 47405	Mathew May	Backpacking	(812) 855-2231
Kaibab Trails Inc. 391 S. Main St. Moab, UT 84532	Jessica Stabrylla	Day Hiking	(801) 259-7423
Moneypenny Expeditions 18950 Marsh Ln. #613 Dallas, TX 75287	Trina Moneypenny	Backpacking	(972) 862-1811
MountainFIT Inc. PO Box 6188 Bozeman, MT 59771	James Healy	Day Hiking	(406) 585-3506
MVP Treks LLC PO Box 490 Sunnydale, UT 84539	Kenneth Salt	Day Hiking	(435) 888-0129
National Outdoor Leadership School 502 Lincoln St. Lander, WY 82520	Willy Cunningham	Backpacking	(307) 332-1416

Northern Arizona University Outdoors PO Box 5773 Flagstaff, AZ 86011	Max Parti	Backpacking	(520) 523-3229
National Outdoor Leadership School, Southwest Ranch 2751 N. Soldier Trail Tucson, AZ 85750	Willie Williams	Backpacking	(520) 749-0955
Outwest Global Adventures PO Box 2050 Red Lodge, MT 59068	Jim Williams	Day Hiking	(406) 446-1533
Peak Performance Assoc., Inc. 630 N. Tejon Colorado Springs, CO 80903	Julie Susemihl	Day Hiking	(719) 633-0804
Pedal the Parks PO Box 455 Cannon Falls, MN 55009	Don Huago	Bicycling	(800) 983-3263
Sierra Club Outings 7620 E. Placita del Pajaro Tucson, AZ 85750	Barry Morenz	Backpacking	(520) 626-6325
Sierrazoza Backpacking Services 1339 N. 64th St. Mesa, AZ 85204	Bill Baker	Day Hiking	(602) 396-4926
Sky Island Treks 928 S. Seventh Ave. Tucson, AZ 85701	Eb Eberlein	Backpacking	(520) 622-6966
Telluride Academy PO Box 2255 Telluride, CO 81435	Wendy Jacobs	Backpacking	(970) 728-5311
Teton Mountain Bike Tours PO Box 7027 Jackson, WY 83002	David F. Hunger	Bicycling	(307) 733-0712
The World Outside 2840 Wilderness Pl., Suite F Boulder, CO 80301	Brian Mullis	Day Hiking Bicycling	(303) 413-0938

Timberline Adventures 7975 E. Harvard, Unit J Denver, CO 80231	Dick Gottsegen	Day Hiking	(303) 759-3804
Trans Group LLC 220 E. Flamingo 2-232 Las Vegas, NV 89109	Kei Takano	Backpacking	(702) 733-6094
University of Calgary Outdoor Program Center 2500 University Dr. N.W. Calgary, Alberta Canada T2N1N4	Jane Papenhuyzen	Backpacking	(403) 220-3695
University of California, Davis, Outdoor Adventures Program 1 Shields Ave. Davis, CA 95616	Dennis Johnson	Backpacking	(530) 752-4362
University of Nebraska, Lincoln PO Box 880232 Lincoln, NE 68588	Martha Christiansen	Backpacking	(402) 472-4761
Western Spirit Cycling 478 Mill Creek Rd. Moab, UT 84532	Ashley Korenblat	Day Hiking	(435) 259-8732
Willard's Adventure Club PO Box 579 Bracebridge, Ontario Canada P1L1T8	Willard Kinzie	Backpacking	(888) 290-9884
Woman Tours PO Box 931 Driggs, ID 83422	Gloria Smith	Bicycling	(208) 354-8804

WHITE-WATER RAFTING COMPANIES

COMPANY	PHONE AND FAX
Aramark-Wilderness River Adventures PO Box 717 Page, AZ 86004	(800) 992-8022 (520) 645-3296 FAX: (520) 645-6113
Arizona Raft Adventures, Inc. 4050 E. Huntington Dr. Flagstaff, AZ 86004	(800) 786-7238 (520) 526-8200 FAX: (520) 526-8246
Arizona River Runners, Inc. PO Box 47788 Phoenix, AZ 85068	(800) 477-7238 (602) 867-4866 FAX: (602) 867-2174
Canyoneers, Inc. PO Box 2997 Flagstaff, AZ 86003	(800) 525-0924 (520) 526-0924 FAX: (520) 527-9398
Canyon Explorations, Inc. PO Box 310 Flagstaff, AZ 86002	(800) 654-0723 (520) 774-4559 FAX: (520) 774-4655
Colorado River & Trail Expeditions, Inc. PO Box 57575 Salt Lake City, UT 84157	(800) 253-7328 (801) 261-1789 FAX : (801) 268-1193
Diamond River Adventures, Inc. PO Box 1316 Page, AZ 86040	(800) 343-3121 (520) 645-8866 FAX: (520) 645-9536
Expeditions, Inc. 625 N. Beaver St. Flagstaff, AZ 86001	(520) 779-3769 FAX: (520) 774-4001
Grand Canyon Expeditions Co. PO Box 0 Kanab, UT 84741	(800) 544-2691 (801) 644-2691 FAX: (801) 644-2699
Hatch River Expeditions, Inc. PO Box 1200 Vernal, UT 84078	(800) 433-8966 (801) 789-3813 FAX: (801) 789-4126
High Desert Adventures, Inc. PO Box 40 St. George, UT 84771	(800) 673-1733 (801) 673-1733 FAX: (801) 673-6696

Hualapai River Runners*
PO Box 246
Peach Springs, AZ 86434

(800) 622-4409
(520) 769-2210
(520) 769-2219
FAX: (520) 769-2637

Mark Sleight Expeditions, Inc.
PO Box 40
St. George, UT 84771

(801) 673-1200

Moki Mac River Expeditions, Inc.
PO Box 71242
Salt Lake City, UT 84171

(800) 284-7280
(801) 268-6667
FAX: (801) 262-0935

OARS/Grand Canyon Dories
PO Box 67
Angels Camp, CA 95222

(800) 346-6277
(209) 736-4677
Dories: (209) 736-2924
FAX: (209) 736-2902

Outdoors Unlimited
6900 Townsend-Winona Road
Flagstaff, AZ 86004

(800) 637-7238
(520) 526-6185
FAX: (520) 526-6185

Tour West, Inc.
PO Box 333
Orem, UT 84059

(800) 453-9107
(801) 225-0755
FAX: (801) 225-7979

Western River Expeditions
7258 Racquet Club Dr.
Salt Lake City, UT 84121

(800) 453-7450
(801) 942-6669
FAX: (801) 942-8514

*Hualapai River Runners is not a National Park Service concessionaire and is not regulated by the National Park Service.

The Alligator: This low-lying ridge is named for its shape, which resembles the silhouette of an alligator.

Apache Point: Named for the Apache Indians of Arizona.

Asbestos Canyon: John Hance and William Ashurst discovered an asbestos vein here in the late 1800s.

Ayer Point: Located near Hance Canyon. Mrs. Edward E. Ayer was the first white woman to visit the Grand Canyon (1885) and travel down into the Canyon via the Hance Trail.

Bass Camp: Named after local legend William Wallace Bass (1841–1933), who set up camp here during his search for trails into the Canyon in 1884. He went on to build guest houses, ferry crossings, and copper and asbestos mines in the Canyon.

Bass Tomb: When Bass died in 1933, he left orders for his body to be cremated and his ashes scattered over Holy Grail Temple, or Bass Tomb.

Beale Point: Named for Lt. Edward Fitzgerald Beale, who in 1857–1858 was in charge of the survey party for a wagon road along the 35th Parallel. Beale used camels for pack animals.

Bedivere Point: Inspired by scenery that resembled places described in the Holy Grail legends, Richard T. Evans in 1902 named parts of the Canyon after characters from Arthurian legends. Some places thus named include Bedivere Point, King Arthur Castle, Lancelot Point, Merlin Abyss, and Mordred Abyss.

Boucher Creek: Named in honor of Louis D. Boucher, who arrived at the Grand Canyon in 1891 and established one of the first tourist camps.

Boulder Creek: What else are you going to call a creek filled with boulders?

Boysag Point: This point, located at the North Rim, is accessible only by a small artificial bridge, hence the Piute word for bridge, *boysag*.

Brahma Temple: Fantastic natural formations gave rise to mystical names, like this corruption of the Hindu word for prayer or supreme creator of the Universe.

Breezy Point: When early residents Emery C. and Ellsworth Kolb stood at this point, the breeze was so strong it lifted gravel from the ground.

Bright Angel Creek: On August 16, 1869, after enduring four straight days of rain, mudslides and flooding, the expedition party of Major

John Wesley Powell came upon a peaceful, clear little creek he named "Bright Angel" (in contrast to the Dirty Devil River in Utah).

Buddha Temple: This feature of the Canyon was so named because it resembles a Buddhist temple. This name was in use as early as 1900.

Burro Canyon: Thousands of wild burros used to flock to this canyon for water. It was also the name of a local Indian family.

Cape Final: In 1880, Major Clarence E. Dutton came to the end of a five-mile ride that left him at this spot gazing out over the Canyon. Dutton said, "It is doubtless the most interesting spot on the Kaibab."

Cape Royal: This point was named by Major Clarence E. Dutton in 1882. In his words, it is a "congregation of wonderful structures, countless and vast, profound lateral chasms."

Cardenas Butte: García López de Cárdenas was a member of the Coronado expedition of 1540 that searched for the Seven Cities of Cibola. Sent to look for a "great canyon," he became the first white man known to have seen the Grand Canyon.

Chemehuevi Point: Named for Chemehuevi Indians, a branch of the Piute tribe.

Cheops Pyramid: Named for Cheops, the Egyptian pharaoh who built the Great Pyramid. George Wharton James says that Cheops Pyramid at the Grand Canyon has a "peculiar shape as of some quaint and Oriental device of symbolic significance."

Chuar Butte: Chuar is short for the name Chuarrumpeak, who was a young chief of the Kaibab Paiute tribe in the 1870s.

Cochise Butte: This butte was named for Cochise, chief of the Chircahua Apaches in the 1860s to early 1870s.

Colorado River: The name is said to come from a Spanish word meaning "red," probably because of the reddish color of the earth around the great river. As far as we know, it was first called this by a Spanish assistant to Father Kino in 1699.

Comanche Point: Originally called "Bissel Point" by George Wharton James in the late 1800s, it was later renamed by the U.S. Geographic Board in honor of the tribe of Plains Indians.

Confucius Temple: Confucius (551–478 B.C.) was the most famous sage of China. This natural formation is another instance of fanciful resemblance to temples associated with the prophets and founders of world religions.

Cope Butte: Edward Drinker Cope (1840–1897) was a noted American paleontologist. In the 1870s he investigated the cretaceous and tertiary strata of the West.

Coronado Butte: In 1540, Francisco Vásquez de Coronado was the leader of a mission to explore the Southwest in search of the Seven Cities of Cibola, a mythical place of unlimited riches. He instead found the mud and stone Zuni villages. He returned to Mexico disheartened and empty-handed.

Cremation Creek: This creek lies at the bottom of Cremation Point (the second above Yavapai Point), where tribal legends speak of funeral cremations and the spreading of ashes over cliffs.

Crystal Creek: A creek with famously clear water, where the first pilots to fly into the Grand Canyon searched for a missing honeymooning couple who perished while boating through the Canyon in 1927.

Dana Butte: This butte was named for American geologist James Dwight Dana (1813–1895). Dana, a professor of geology at Yale University, wrote more than two hundred scientific books and papers.

Darwin Plateau: This plateau was named for Charles Darwin, the evolutionist and British naturalist who proposed species changed through natural selection.

DeMotte Park: This open glade on the Kaibab Plateau was named by Major John Wesley Powell in August 1872, for his friend Dr. Harvey C. DeMotte, professor of mathematics at Wesleyan University and fellow expedition member.

Deubendorff Rapids: Deubendorff, a boatman for the 1909 Galloway-Stone Expedition, capsized in these rapids. The four-boat expedition ran from Green River, Wyoming, to Needles, California in two months and one week, the fastest on record.

Devil's Corkscrew: This portion of the Bright Angel Trail is so named because it winds and twists downward for twelve hundred feet.

Dunn Butte: William H. Dunn was a member of Major John Wesley Powell's first Colorado River expedition in 1869.

Dutton Point: Named for Major Clarence E. Dutton, a famous geologist and author of *The Tertiary History of the Grand Canyon*

District (1882). Dutton was responsible for many place names in the Grand Canyon.

Elves Chasm: This chasm contains fantastic forms of travertine and wildflowers of columbine and orchids. A trip into this beautiful little canyon is like a visit to Fairyland.

Escalante Creek: Named by Major John Wesley Powell in honor of the daring adventurer Father Silvestre Velez de Escalante, who crossed the Colorado River in the late 1700s.

Farview Point: Near Point Imperial. There is a broad view of the Painted Desert from this point.

Galloway Canyon: Nathaniel Galloway was a Mormon trapper who floated down the Colorado through the Canyon on two expeditions around the turn of the century.

Garces Terrace: Named for Father Francisco Garces, who in 1775 made contact with the Havasupai and other tribes south of the Grand Canyon. In 1781, while serving as priest at the mission near what is now Yuma, he was killed by Indians.

Garden Creek: At the lower end of this creek, Indians ran irrigation ditches for their gardens, hence the name.

Grand Canyon Village: This is the main tourist accommodation point and park administration area for the Grand Canyon.

Grandview Trail: The Grandview Trail was completed in 1893 by Pete Berry, who built the trail for access to his copper mine. The name, also used for the Grandview Hotel in 1904 and Grandview Caves in 1897, derives from the obvious: one heck of a view.

Granite Gorge: Large masses of pink and white granite give this 40-mile gorge its name. It covers river miles 77 to 118.

Great Thumb Point: So named because its shape resembles a large thumb from above.

Greenland Spring: This spring lies on what is known as the Greenland or Walhalla Plateau. Walhalla Plateau has been the official name since 1902, but before that Mormon cattlemen referred to the plateau as Greenland.

Hakatai Canyon: *Hakatai* is the Havasupai name for the Colorado River, meaning a large roaring sound.

Hance Creek: Hance Creek was named for John Hance (1839–1919), a legendary pioneer and resident of the South Rim in the late 1800s. He paved the way for visitors to see the Canyon, and spun wild tales of digging out the Canyon himself and using the dirt to build the San Francisco Peaks.

Hancock Butte: Named after Captain William Augustus Hancock (1831–1902), surveyor, post trader, and sheriff in southern Arizona.

Hansbrough Point: Peter Hansbrough was an ill-fated member of the Robert Brewster Stanton expedition of 1889. He drowned after his boat capsized, and was buried at the point that bears his name.

Havasu Canyon: The Havasupai Indians lived in and around the Grand Canyon. Havasu comes from the Indian words *haha,* "water" and *vasu,* "blue," and translates as "blue water."

Hermit Basin: This area was named after Louis Boucher, "The Hermit," a reclusive French-Canadian who established a camp to provide sleeping and eating accommodations for tourists who came down the trail to the Colorado River bed. His was the first provision for travelers near the river.

Hillers Butte: John K. Hillers was a photographer on the second Grand Canyon expedition under Major John Wesley Powell in 1871–1872.

Hindu Amphitheater: In 1882 Major Clarence E. Dutton wrote that this natural amphitheater was marked by its "profusion and richness [which] suggests an oriental character."

Hopi Point: This point was named for the Hopi Indians, who live on the Hopi Reservation. Their name is translated as the "Peaceful People."

Howlands Butte: Brothers Seneca and O. G. Howland were members of Major John Wesley Powell's first Grand Canyon expedition in 1869. After encountering the severity of the Colorado River rapids, they left the party, climbed up the Canyon, and were killed by Indians on Shivwits Plateau.

Hualapai Canyon: The Hualapai Indians live today on a reservation south of the Canyon. Some early histories describe them as a fierce tribe in the early territorial days of Arizona.

Hubbell Butte: Juan Lorenzo Hubbell (1853–1930) settled on the Navajo Indian Reservation at Ganado, Arizona in 1871 as a pioneer trader. He also served as county sheriff and in the state senate.

Imperial Point (Point Imperial): This is the highest point along either rim of the Grand Canyon. Its lofty status may have inspired the name "imperial."

Indian Garden: According to George Wharton James, this spot had been cultivated by a Havasupai family years before white men set eyes on it. It is today a resting point for those who make the descent into the Canyon along Bright Angel Trail.

Isis Temple: George Wharton James said that this temple-like formation was named for the goddess of the Egyptians, and that in front of it are two notable great cloisters.

Ives Point: Lieutenant Joseph Christmas Ives was the first military man to explore the Colorado River to its headwaters for navigational purposes. In 1851 he made a surveying trip from west to east across Arizona.

Johnson Point: Fred Johnson was a Grand Canyon National Park ranger who drowned in 1929 at Horn Creek Rapid while performing official duties.

Kaibab Plateau: In 1874, Major John Wesley Powell noted that the great plateau forming the North Rim of the Grand Canyon was called by the Indians *Kai-vav-wi,* "a mountain lying down." In English this became Kaibab Plateau. The Paiutes refer to the great forests lying on this plateau as the *Kaibabits.*

Kanab Canyon: From the Paiute word for "willow." Kanab Canyon was where the exhausted Powell expedition received sorely needed rations from team packers Joe Hamblin, George Adair, and Nathan Adams, who had traveled down the Canyon and waited for the explorers.

Kanab Creek: Many willow trees along this creek gave it its name.

Kolb (Natural) Bridge: Named for Emery C. Kolb, who with his brother Ellsworth became famous for his photographs and explorations of the Grand Canyon. The name was suggested by Senator Barry Goldwater.

Kwagunt Valley: In 1869, this valley was named by Major John Wesley Powell after a Paiute Indian named Quagunt (or Kwagunt), who was very friendly to the exploring party. The Paiute Indians said that Quagunt owned the valley, which was a gift from his father.

Lava Falls: The Powell expedition of 1871 observed that the Canyon appeared to have once been filled with lava to a depth of 1,500 feet. They named the descent Lava Falls.

Lipan Point: The first mention of the Lipan Indians occurred in 1699, when they were named as allies of the Comanches. In 1902, the name of this point was changed from Lincoln to Lipan.

Lyell Butte: Sir Charles Lyell (1798–1875) was a British geologist whose noted work, *The Principles of Geology,* published in 1830 and 1832, was a direct forerunner of the theory of evolution advanced by Charles Darwin.

Manzanita Point: This point was named by Colonel John White, a Canyon resident in the 1920s. On one visit to the North Rim, he ascended Bright Angel Creek and noticed a large manzanita bush. There he wrote on a piece of wood "Manzanita Point."

Marble Gorge: On August 9, 1869, Major John Wesley Powell wrote that his exploring party passed between cliffs of marble in which were a great number of caves. He named the gorge Marble Canyon.

Maricopa Point: This point was named to honor the Maricopa Indians, a tribe living in south central Arizona, noted for friendliness to white settlers.

Marsh Butte: George Wharton James named this place for the American paleontologist Othniel Charles Marsh (1831–1899). Marsh investigated fossils of the western United States, among them the early ancestors of horses.

Matkatamiba Canyon: *Matkatamiba* is the name of an old Havasupai Indian family.

Matthes Point: In 1902, Francois E. Matthes was in charge of making the first topographic map of the Grand Canyon. He was responsible for many of the names based on mythological deities following Clarence Dutton's lead.

Mohave Point: The Mohave Indians lived along the Colorado River. Their name, meaning "three mountains," came from the fact that the tribe lived near the Needles, a group of three sharp peaks located in Mohave County, Arizona. The town of Needles was relocated across the river in California.

Monument Creek: A single shaft, about 100 feet high and resembling a great monument, is visible from the rim at this point.

Moran Point: Thomas Moran was an artist who first visited the North Rim in 1873 with Major John Wesley Powell. Although his paintings of the Grand Canyon were largely responsible for making the American public aware of the wonders of the Grand Canyon, the point is actually named for his brother Peter who accompanied the Bourke 1881 expedition as an artist.

Mount Hayden: Charles Trumbull Hayden came to Arizona in 1857 on the first Butterfield Overland Stage. In 1870 he established Hayden's Ferry, now called Tempe.

Muav Canyon: This canyon was probably named after a Paiute word meaning "divide" or "pass" because of the presence of the Muav Saddle, a pass in the canyon rim at the top of the north wall. Powell spoke of it by this name in 1869.

Nankoweap Butte: The word means "place where Indians had a fight," which is apparently what happened here at some point in Canyon history (an Apache attack on Kaibab Paiute).

Neal Spring: This spring at the head of Bright Angel Canyon was named for a local cowpuncher.

140-Mile Canyon: The Powell Grand Canyon expeditions named several canyons according to their distance from the party's entrance to the Grand Canyon.

O'Neill Spring: This spring on Horseshoe Mesa was named for Jim O'Neill, a scout for General George Crook.

Osiris Temple: Another one of the fancifully named features, this one for the chief deity of the ancient Egyptian pantheon.

Paiute Point: A lookout named for the Paiute Indians, the tribe native to the area north of the Grand Canyon.

Palisades of the Desert: These bold cliffs are at the western border of the Painted Desert. The name was proposed by Francois E. Matthes in 1902.

Papago Point: This point was named for the Papago tribe of southern and southwestern Arizona and northern Sonora.

Paya Point: This point was named for Lemuel Paya, a Havasupai Indian, once a member of the Supai Tribal Council.

Phantom Ranch: The Phantom Ranch is the only area at the bottom of the Grand Canyon with guest accommodations. Once called Rust Camp, it was renamed by Mary Colter for its haze that creates an illusory effect on the narrow gorge.

Pima Point: A lookout named for the Pima Indians, a peaceful, agricultural tribe living in south central Arizona.

Point Sublime: Major Clarence E. Dutton spent many hours on this point, writing descriptions of Grand Canyon scenery. He is said to have called it "the most sublime of the earthly spectacles." He named the promontory in 1880.

Powell Plateau: In 1869, Major John Wesley Powell led the first successful Euro-American exploration of the Canyon's towering walls and dangerous rapids, and named it the Grand Canyon. In 1871–1872, Powell again explored the Canyon, making scientific records. Powell later became the first director of the U.S. Geological Survey and of the U.S. Bureau of American Ethnology. A monument at Powell Point (Powell Point Memorial) commemorates his achievements in the Grand Canyon. The plateau was named in 1882 by Clarence Dutton.

Putesoi Canyon: *Putesoi* is the name of a Havasupai Indian family.

Ribbon Falls: Beneath the North Rim, this single fall drops down in a cut from an overhang and makes a moss-green, ribbonlike track against the red wall of the Canyon.

Roaring Springs: These springs at the head of Bright Angel Creek gush with such force from the Canyon wall that they make a true roaring sound. The water then plunges 400 feet down a fern-covered slope.

Rowe Well: In June 1890, Sanford Rowe, a pioneer stockman and guide, began digging here in search of underground water. He later developed Rowe Well into an auto camp.

Santa Maria Spring: This spring, about 1,760 feet below Hermit Trailhead, was named by Mary Colter, the architect for many of the South Rim buildings—the Lookout, Hermits Rest, and the Watchtower.

Sapphire Canyon: Major John Wesley Powell named this canyon for its coloring.

Shinumo Altar: Named by Frederick Dellenbaugh, who thought the 600-foot formation resembled a great altar. *Shinumo* comes from the Paiute Indian name for the area's earliest residents.

Shiva Temple: Shiva Temple is a wooded butte that was once part of the North Rim. It was named after a Hindu god by Major Clarence E. Dutton in 1880. He described it as "the grandest of all the buttes, and the most majestic in aspect, though not the most ornate."

Shoshone Point: Named for the Shoshone Indian tribe of northwest Wyoming.

Sinking Ship: The tilting of the strata in this formation gives it the appearance of a sinking ship.

Sinyala Canyon: George Wharton James's favored guide was a Havasupai named Sinyala.

60-Mile Creek: This creek is about sixty miles below Lees Ferry. Apparently this name was suggested by Francois E. Matthes, Richard F. Evans, and J. R. Evans.

Sockdolager Rapids: *Sockdolager* is 1800s British and American slang for "heavy or knock-down blow" or a "finisher." It is the word chosen by Powell's expedition team to describe a particularly awesome set of rapids that had them shaking in their boots.

Stanton Point: This point was named by Robert Brewster Stanton (1846–1922), who headed an 1890 boat expedition down the Colorado River in Grand Canyon to study the feasibility of a railroad along the canyon floor.

Sturdevant Point: Glen E. Sturdevant was a park naturalist who drowned in the Colorado River just below this point in 1929.

Supai: This is the official name for the Havasupai village that is the center of tribal activities. A "Supai" reservation was created on June 8, 1880, but the area later underwent changes, with the present 518 acres being set aside on March 31, 1882 for the "Yavai Suppai" Indians. This village is subject to severe floods. In 1910 a rim-to-rim, forty-foot wall of water swept away all buildings while the Indians clung to the cliffsides and watched the raging torrent. Today, an estimated 235 Havasupai live on the reservation. The tribe also has rights to 2,540 acres in Cataract Canyon.

Tanner Canyon: In 1889, Seth B. Tanner helped build a trail from the South Rim down into the Canyon to the Colorado River, to reach his mining claims.

Thor's Hammer: George Wharton James said that he named this formation because of its resemblance to a hammer huge enough to be used by the Norse god Thor.

Tilted Mesa: Francois E. Matthes suggested this name for the sloping tableland west of Marble Gorge, on the Kaibab Monocline.

Toltec Point: The name derives from an archaeological theory, which posited that Toltec Indians from Mexico had contacts as far north as the Gila River in Arizona.

Tonto Trail: This trail is on the South Rim on the Tonto Platform. It was named for the so-called Tonto Apaches, a term that included members of several tribes.

Tovar Terrace: Named after Pedro de Tobar (or Tovar), an aristocratic member of the 1540 Coronado expedition, who learned of the Grand Canyon in his conversations with Hopi Indians. When he reported this to Coronado, Cárdenas was sent to investigate.

Tower of Ra: In ancient Egyptian mythology, Ra was the god of the sun, a principal deity. The pharaohs claimed to be Ra's incarnations.

Tower of Set: Set was the Egyptian god of war. This location was named by the artist Thomas Moran in 1879.

The Transept: Major Clarence E. Dutton wrote in 1882 that this portion of the Grand Canyon's North Rim is "the finest and most picturesque of the gorges of the Kaibab front . . . far grander than Yosemite."

Travertine Canyon: Waters heavily charged with calcium carbonate leave a deposit of smooth, soft green stone called travertine. Seepage has deposited travertine all over this canyon wall. There are actually two such canyons, at river miles 95.5 and 229.

Tusayan Ruin: This small ruin, once inhabited by pueblo dwellers around 1200 A. D., lies behind the Tusayan Museum on the South Rim of the Grand Canyon. Spaniards used the name *Tusayan* for the Hopi mesas and villages.

Upset Rapids: In 1923, the USGS Birdseye expedition mapping the Grand Canyon had its first boat upset in this hitherto-unnamed location.

Vasey's Paradise: George W. Vasey (1822–1893) served as a botanist with the United States Department of Agriculture from 1872–1893. He was a valuable member of Powell's expedition to the Rocky Mountains in 1868.

Vishnu Temple: The Hindu god Vishnu is a a member of the supreme trinity, along with Brahman and Shiva. The butte was named in 1880 by Major Clarence E. Dutton.

Vista Encantadora: In 1941, the original name of *Vista Encantada* ("enchanted view") was boldly changed by Park Supervisor Dr. Harold C. Bryant to Vista Encantadora ("enchanting view") to be gramatically correct.

Watahomigi Point: This point is located on the South Rim, 1½ miles south of Havasu Falls. It was named for a Havasupai Indian family.

Wescogame Point: This point was named for a Havasupai Indian family whose members still live nearby.

Widforss Point: In December 1937, this point was named to honor Gunnar Mauritz Widforss, an artist whose Canyon paintings remain some of the best ever done. He died on the canyon rim in 1943.

Yaki Point: This point was named just prior to 1910, when the Yaqui Indians of Mexico were struggling with the Mexican government against being transported from their home in northern Mexico. Many Yaquis fled to the United States for refuge.

Yavapai Point: Named for the Yavapai Indians of Arizona, actually Apache–Mohave who lived along Arizona's Verde River.

Yuma Point: The Yuma Indians inhabit the lower reaches of the Colorado River where Yuma, Arizona, is today.

Zoroaster Temple: Named after Zoroaster, the founder of the ancient national religion of the Perso-Iranian people. Both G. W. James and Clarence Dutton used this name for this formation.

Zuni Point: This point was named for a tribe of Indians which lives in New Mexico near the Arizona border, northeast of Springerville. The "seven cities of Cibola" were thought by the Spanish to be in the Zuni homeland.

Partially excerpted from Grand Canyon Place Names, *by Byrd H. Granger (University of Arizona Press, 1960; annotated and enlarged by Sara T. Stebbins, 1999).*

GETTING THERE

AMTRAK Corporation . . . .(800) 872-7245
Current road conditions for No. Arizona . . . .(520) 779-2711
Educational fee waivers . . . .(520) 638-7850
Grand Canyon Airport . . . .(520) 638-2463
Grand Canyon Railway . . . .(800) 843-8724 or (520) 773-1976
Grand Canyon/Tusayan Shuttle (Cassi Tours) . . . . . .(520) 638-0821
Gray Line of Flagstaff (Nava-Hopi Tours)
. . . .(800) 892-8687 or (520) 774-5003
Greyhound Bus Line . . . .(800) 231-2222
National Park Service Grand Canyon information . .(520) 638-7888
Transportation Desk: North Rim . . . .(520) 638-2612
Transportation Desk: South Rim . . . .(520) 638-2631

PARK ATTRACTIONS

Backcountry Office: South Rim . . . .(520) 638-7875
Desert View Watchtower Information Center . . . .(520) 638-2736
Havasupai Tourist Enterprise . . . .(520) 448-2121
North Rim Visitor Center . . . .(520) 638-7864
Tusayan Ruin & Museum . . . .(520) 638-2305

GETTING AROUND

Grand Canyon Field Institute study trips . . . .(520) 638-2485
Grand Canyon Motorcoach Tours
. . . .(520) 638-2631 or (303) 297-2757
Grand Canyon Railway . . . .(800) 843-8724
    International callers . . . .(520) 773-1976
Grand Canyon road information (24-hour) . . . .(520) 638-7888
Grand Canyon Taxi . . . .(520) 638-2822 or 638-2631, ext. 6563
Gray Line of Flagstaff (Nava-Hopi Tours) . . . .(800) 892-8687
North Kaibab Ranger Station (North Rim) . . . .(520) 643-7395
South Rim Travel . . . .(888) 291-9116
Transcanyon Shuttle . . . .(520) 638-2820
Tusayan Ranger Station (South Rim) . . . .(520) 638-2443
Air Tours:
Air Grand Canyon Family Tours . . . .(520) 638-2686
Air Star Airlines . . . .(520) 638-2139
Airwest Helicopters of Arizona . . . .(520) 516-2790
Kenai Helicopters . . . .(520) 638-2764
Papillon Grand Canyon Helicopters
. . . .(800) 528-2418 or (520) 638-2419

TELEPHONE DIRECTORY

LODGING AND DINING
Grand Canyon National Park Lodges (Amfac Parks & Resorts):
Advance reservations . . . .(303) 29-PARKS (297-2757)
Same-day reservations . . . .(520) 638-2631

Delaware North Parks Services Stores
(formerly Babbitt's) . . . .(520) 638-2262
Dining in nearby towns .(see Lodging and Dining, pages 101–104)
Grand Canyon Kennels . . . .(520) 638-0534
Grand Canyon Music Festival . . . .(800) 997-8285 or (520) 638-9215
Lodgings outside the park . .(see Lodging and Dining, pages 94–98)

CAMPING AND BACKPACKING
Camping Reservations Inside Park:
Mather Campground (South Rim) . . . .(800) 365-2267
North Rim Campground . . . .(800) 365-2267
Trailer Village (South Rim) . . . .(303) 29-PARKS (297-2757)

Camping Outside Park:
Camper Village (Tusayan) . . . .(520) 638-2887
DeMotte Campground (North Rim) . . . .(520) 643-7395
Jacob Lake Campground (North Rim) . . . .(520) 643-7395
Kaibab Camper Village (North Rim) . . . .(520) 643-7395
Kaibab National Forest (North Rim) . . . .(520) 643-7395
Kaibab National Forest (South Rim) . . . .(520) 638-2443
Ten-X Campground . . . .(520) 638-2443
Tuweep Ranger Station . . . .(520) 716-2843

Other Useful Numbers:
Backcountry Information Center (South Rim) . . . .(520) 638-7875
Grand Canyon Field Institute . . . .(520) 638-2485

RECREATIONAL OPPORTUNITIES
Mule & Horseback Riding:
Horseback trail rides: outside park, South Rim
. . . .(520) 638-2891 or 638-2424
Mule & horse trips: outside park, North Rim . . . . .(435) 644-8150
Mule trips: inside park, North Rim . . . .(435) 679-8665
Mule trips: inside park, South Rim . . . .(303) 29-PARKS (297-2757)
Western Grand Canyon: Hualapai Hilltop
. . . .(520) 448-2121 or 448-2111

River Trips:
Smooth-water trips (information) . . . .(800) 528-6154
White-water trips . . . .(see Outfitters List, pages 191–192)

Fishing:
Lees Ferry Anglers, Lees Ferry . . . .(520) 355-2261
Marble Canyon Lodge & Outfitters, Lees Ferry . . . .(520) 355-2225
Phantom Ranch . . . .(520) 638-2631
Ranger Office, Lake Mead Recreation Area . . . . . .(520) 767-3401

Bicycle Shops:
Absolute Bikes, Flagstaff . . . .(520) 779-5969
Cosmic Cycles, Flagstaff . . . .(520) 779-1092
Desert Jeep & Bike Rentals, Sedona . . . .(520) 284-1099
Mountain Bike Heaven, Sedona . . . .(520) 282-1312
Sedona Bike & Bean Shoppe, Sedona . . . .(520) 282-3515
Sedona Sports, Sedona . . . .(520) 282-1317
Sedona Sports Chalet, Sedona . . . .(520) 282-6956

Winter Activities:
Inner Canyon . . . .(520) 638-2631
North Kaibab Ranger District (North Rim) . . . .(520) 643-7395
Tusayan Ranger District (South Rim) . . . .(520) 638-2443

AMERICAN INDIAN RESERVATIONS
Havasupai Tourist Enterprise . . . .(520) 448-2121
Hopi Cultural Center . . . .(520) 734-2401
Hualapai Tribal Enterprises . . . .(520) 769-2419
Kaibab Paiute Cultural Office . . . .(520) 643-6014
Navajo Nation Parks and Recreation . . . .(520) 871-6645

AREA ATTRACTIONS
Arboretum at Flagstaff . . . .(520) 774-1442
Canyon de Chelly National Monument . . . .(520) 674-5500
Glen Canyon National Recreation Area . . . .(520) 608-6404
Lowell Observatory, Flagstaff . . . .(520) 774-2096
Meteor Crater . . . .(520) 289-5898
Montezuma Castle National Monument . . . .(520) 567-5276
Monument Valley Navajo Tribal Park . . . .(520) 672-2366
Museum of Northern Arizona, Flagstaff . . . .(520) 774-5213
Sunset Crater National Monument . . . .(520) 556-7134
Tuzigoot National Monument . . . .(520) 634-5564
Walnut Canyon National Monument . . . .(520) 526-1157
Wupatki National Monument . . . .(520) 526-1157

ENVIRONMENTAL EDUCATION AND PRESERVATION
Arizona Fish & Game Department . . . .(520) 774-5045
Grand Canyon Association . . . . .(800) 858-2808 or (520) 638-2481
Grand Canyon Field Institute . . . .(520) 638-2485
Grand Canyon National Park Foundation . . . .(520) 774-1760
Grand Canyon Trust . . . .(888) GCT-5550 or (520) 774-7488
NPS Environmental Education Programs . . . .(520) 638-7762
Peregrine Fund . . . .(520) 355-2270

VISITOR SERVICES IN SURROUNDING AREA
Flagstaff, Arizona (Chamber of Commerce) . . . .(520) 774-4504
Flagstaff Visitor Center . . . .(520) 774-9541 or (800) 842-7293
Kanab, Utah (Chamber of Commerce)
. . . .(801) 644-5033 or (800) 733-5263
Page, Arizona (Chamber of Commerce) . . . .(520) 645-2741
Sedona, Arizona (Chamber of Commerce)
. . . .(520) 282-7722 or (800) 288-7336
Tusayan, Arizona (Chamber of Commerce) . . . .(520) 638-2901
Williams, Arizona (Chamber of Commerce) . . . .(520) 635-4061

Averages measured in Fahrenheit and inches

	SOUTH RIM			INNER CANYON			NORTH RIM		
	Max	Min	Prec	Max	Min	Prec	Max	Min	Prec
January	41	18	1.32	56	36	.68	37	16	3.17
February	45	21	1.55	62	42	.75	39	18	3.22
March	51	25	1.38	71	48	.79	44	21	2.63
April	60	32	.93	82	56	.47	53	29	1.73
May	70	39	.66	92	63	.36	62	34	1.17
June	81	47	.42	101	72	.30	73	40	.86
July	84	54	1.81	106	78	.84	77	46	1.93
August	82	53	2.25	103	75	1.40	75	45	2.85
September	76	47	1.56	97	69	.97	69	39	1.99
October	65	36	1.10	84	58	.65	59	31	1.38
November	52	27	.94	68	46	.43	46	24	1.48
December	43	20	1.62	57	37	.87	40	20	2.83

WHERE CAN WE FIND A GAS STATION?

Grand Canyon Chevron operates one service station on the South Rim at Desert View, located 25 miles east of the Village. Desert View Chevron is open April through September only. Just outside the south entrance to the park, you'll find Moqui Texaco located at Moqui Lodge, and a Grand Canyon Union 76 located in Tusayan.

On the North Rim, Grand Canyon Chevron (gasoline and propane fuels, no diesel) operates a service station on the North Rim Campground access road. Hours are 7:00 a.m.–7:00 p.m. daily, May 15–October 15 only. Outside the park, gas stations are located at the Kaibab Lodge (gasoline, diesel, and automotive supplies), 5 miles north of the park entrance, 7:00 a.m.–7:00 p.m., May 15–October 15 only; and the Jacob Lake Inn Chevron (gasoline and propane fuels, no diesel), 32 miles north of the park entrance. The Jacob Lake Inn Chevron is open year round, 6:30 a.m.–9:00 p.m. (summer), and 7:30 a.m.–6:30 p.m. (winter).

WHERE CAN WE FIND TOWING AND REPAIR SERVICES?

The Grand Canyon Garage operates a repair and towing facility located next door to the Grand Canyon National Park Lodges administrative offices in Grand Canyon Village on the South Rim. It's open year-round from 8:00 a.m.–5:00 p.m. daily. Call (520) 638-2631 for 24-hour emergency vehicle towing. On the North Rim, the Grand Canyon Chevron station provides minor repairs (tires, etc.). For all mechanical work, you'll have to go to Judd Auto Service located 75 miles north of the park entrance in Fredonia, Arizona. It's open year-round from 6:00 a.m.–9:00 p.m. (summer), and 8:00 a.m.–6:00 p.m. (winter). Call them at (520) 643-7107.

WHERE CAN WE FIND PUBLIC RESTROOMS?
SHOWERS? LAUNDROMATS?

There are public restrooms at all of the visitor and information centers, and inside all lodging facilities throughout the park. On the South Rim, coin-operated shower and laundry facilities (as well as a public restroom) are located next to Mather Campground (7:00 a.m.–9:00 p.m. in the summer; hours vary in the winter). On the North Rim, you'll find coin-operated laundry and shower facilities near the North Rim Campground (7:00 a.m.–9:00 p.m., May 15–October 15 only).

WHERE CAN WE FIND A POST OFFICE?
The main post office at the Grand Canyon is located in Grand Canyon Village, across from the visitor center. It offers year-round window service Monday–Friday, 9:00 a.m.–4:30p.m. From early May to September, the hours are extended to include Saturday and Sunday, 10:00 a.m.–2:00 p.m. It's closed holidays, but stamps are available from a machine in the lobby, which is open from 5:00 a.m.–10:00 p.m. There's also a post office located just outside the park's south entrance, in Tusayan, in the Delaware North Park Services store (formerly Babbitt's General Store, soon to be renamed). On the North Rim, you'll find a post office in the Grand Canyon Lodge complex, with window service offered 8:00–11:00 a.m. and 11:30–4:00 p.m. (Monday–Friday), and 8:00 a.m.–2:00 p.m. (Saturday). It's closed Sundays and holidays.

WHERE CAN WE FIND A BANK, CASH A CHECK, OR EXCHANGE FOREIGN CURRENCY?
There is a full-service Bank One in Grand Canyon Village, next to the post office and across the street from the visitor center. Hours are 10:00 a.m.–3:00 p.m. (Monday–Thursday), and 10:00 a.m.–3:00 p.m. and 4:00–6:00 p.m. (Friday). It's closed weekends and holidays. The bank will cash traveler's checks, give cash advances on credit cards, and make wire transfers. A 24-hour ATM machine accepts cards from Bank One, American Express, Plus and Star Systems, Arizona Interchange Network, and Master Teller. There are banks in the gateway communities of Williams and Flagstaff, Arizona. The closest bank to the North Rim is located in Kanab, Utah. You can also cash traveler's checks (if you're a hotel guest) at the front desks of most park lodges.

WHERE IS THE LOST AND FOUND?
You can turn in or trace lost and found articles at any visitor center or ranger station, or call (520) 638-2631, ext. 6503 to report items lost or found in lodges, restaurants, or lounges on the South Rim. For all other lost or found items, call (520) 638-7798, from 8:00 a.m.–6:30 p.m. On the North Rim, call the NPS Visitor Center at (520) 638-7864, from May 15–October 15 only.

WHERE CAN WE RECEIVE MEDICAL SERVICES?
Dial 911 for 24-hour emergency fire, medical, or ranger assistance or to report accidents or injuries. On the South Rim, call the Grand Canyon Clinic, (520) 638-2551 or 638-2469; the Pharmacy, (520) 638-

2460; or the Dentist Office, (520) 638-2395. The clinic is located off
Center Road in Grand Canyon Village. Hours are 8:00 a.m.–5:30 p.m.
(Monday–Friday), and 9:00 a.m.–noon (Saturday). The clinic is closed
on Sundays. On the North Rim, there's a clinic located in Cabin
#5, adjacent to the Grand Canyon Lodge complex. A nurse practi-
tioner provides services on a walk-in or appointment basis. Hours are
9:00 a.m.–noon and 3:00–6:00 p.m. (Saturday, Sunday, Monday);
9:00 a.m.–noon and 2:00–5:00 p.m. (Tuesday); closed Wednesday
and Thursday; 9:00 a.m.–noon and 2:00–6:00 p.m. (Friday).

WHERE CAN WE GET A GOLDEN EAGLE PASS OR A GOLDEN AGE PASS?

Golden Eagle Passes (good for all national parks for one year from
the date of purchase) can only be purchased from rangers at park
entrance stations. The cost is $50 annually. Golden Age Passes, which
are lifetime passes to all national parks, can also only be purchased
at park entrance stations, and require a one-time $10 fee when issued
to qualifying senior citizens (U.S. citizens or legal residents, age 62
or older).

WHERE CAN WE FIND THE GRAND CANYON FIELD INSTITUTE OFFICE?

The Institute is headquartered in a large, historic community
building next to the old Mule Barn, and near Maswik Transportation
Center and the Backcountry Information Center in Grand Canyon
Village. Call them at (520) 638-2485, or visit their website at
www.thecanyon.com/fieldinstitute for more information.

WHERE CAN WE FIND THE GRAND CANYON ASSOCIATION OFFICE?

The GCA is headquartered in a building located at 1 Tonto Street in
Grand Canyon Village. Call them at (520) 638-2481, or visit their
website at www.thecanyon.com/gca for more information.

WHERE CAN WE FIND OUT ABOUT SPECIAL VISITOR SERVICES?

The Grand Canyon National Park Accessibility Guide, indicating
the accessibility of most public buildings, park facilities, and trails
to visitors with disabilities, is available free upon request at NPS visitor and information centers. Call (520) 638-7888 for more information, or (520) 638-7804 for TDD.

· Further Reading ·

The Ace in the Hole: A Brief History of Company 818 of the Civilian Conservation Corps by Louis Lester Purvis. Brentwood Christian Press, 1989.

Arizona Road and Recreation Atlas. Benchmark Maps, 1996.

Arizona, the Grand Canyon State by Steven L. Walker. Camelback, 1991.

Bibliography of the Grand Canyon and the Lower Colorado River from 1540 compiled by Earle E. Spamer. Grand Canyon Association, 1990.

Checklist of the Birds, Mammals, Plants, Reptiles & Amphibians of the Grand Canyon Area compiled by Kathy Butterfield et al. Grand Canyon Association, 1993.

Colorado River in Grand Canyon: A Comprehensive Guide to Its Natural and Human History by Larry Stevens. Fifth edition. Red Lake Books, 1998.

The Exploration of the Colorado River and Its Canyons by John Wesley Powell. Dover, 1961.

Exploring the Grand Canyon: Adventures of Yesterday and Today by Lynne Foster. Grand Canyon Association, 1990.

A Field Guide to the Grand Canyon by Stephen Whitney. Second edition. Mountaineers Books, 1996.

Grand Canyon Loop Hikes II by George Steck. Chockstone Press, 1993.

Grand Canyon Magazine. American Park Network, 1998.

Grand Canyon National Park Road Guide by Jeremy Schmidt. Revised edition. Free Wheeling Travel Guides, 1997.

Grand Canyon Place Names by Byrd H. Granger. University of Arizona Press, 1999.

Grand Canyon Wildflowers by Arthur M. Phillips III. Grand Canyon Association, 1996.

A Guide to Grand Canyon National Park and Vicinity by Sandra Scott. Grand Canyon Association, 1997.

A Guide to the Grand Canyon Village by Timothy Manns. Grand Canyon Association, 1996.

Havasuw 'Baaja: People of the Blue Green Water by Stephen Hirst. Havasupai Tribe, 1985.

The Hidden Canyon: A River Journey by John Blaustein. Chronicle Books, 1999.

In the House of Stone and Light: An Introduction to the Human History of Grand Canyon by J. Donald Hughes. Grand Canyon Association, 1993.

An Introduction to Grand Canyon Ecology by Rose Houk. Grand Canyon Association, 1996.

An Introduction to Grand Canyon Geology by L. Greer Price. Grand Canyon Association, 1999.

Kaibab National Forest Maps. U.S. Forest Service, 1994.

Living At The Edge: Explorers, Exploiters and Settlers of the Grand Canyon Region by Michael F. Anderson. Grand Canyon Association, 1998.

The Majesty of the Grand Canyon: 150 Years in Art by Joni Louise Kinsey. First Glance Books, 1998.

Mammals of Grand Canyon by Donald F. Hoffmeister. University of Illinois, 1971.

Mary Colter: Builder Upon the Red Earth by Virginia Graton. Nothland Press, 1980.

Official Guide to Hiking the Grand Canyon by Scott Thybony. Revised edition. Grand Canyon Association, 1997.

On the Edge of Splendor by Douglas W. Schwartz. School of American Research, 1989.

101 Questions About Desert Life by Alice Jablonsky. Southwest Parks and Monuments Association, 1994.

Plateau Journal: Land and Peoples of the Colorado Plateau. The Museum of Northern Arizona and the Grand Canyon Association, (Winter) 1997–1998.

Quest For The Pillar Of Gold: The Mines and Miners of the Grand Canyon by George H. Billingsley and Earle E. Spamer. Grand Canyon Association, 1997.

River Runners of the Grand Canyon by David Lavender. Grand Canyon Association, 1990.

River to Rim by Nancy Brian. Earthquest Press, 1992.

Index

San Francisco Peaks, 54
Sanitary dump facilities.
    See RV sites
Santa Fe Grand Canyon Railway.
    See Grand Canyon Railway
Santa Fe Railway Station, 63, 81, 84
Santa Maria Spring, 86, 201
Sapphire Canyon, 201
School buses, 77
Schools, 12, 77
Scorpions, 43, 124, 131
Seasonal events, 106
Seasons, 8, 9, 10, 16, 88, 118, 148-49, 209
    and crowds, 86
    and fishing, 146
    and hiking, 129, 130
    and plants, 50, 52, 53
    and rafting, 141-42
    and wildlife, 47
    See also specific seasons
Self-guided trails and walks. *See*
    Trails and walks
Service stations, 12, 210
Shinumo Altar, 201
Shiva Temple, 202
Shoshone Point, 202
Shower facilities, 12, 108, 210
Shrine of Ages Building, 80, 114
Shrubs, 51
Shuttle services, 12, 68-69, 73
    airport to park, 6
    between rims, 6, 12, 76
    map, 22
    South Rim, 12, 21, 22, 68-69, 73, 75
    wheelchair accessibility, 73
Sinking Ship (rock formation), 202
Sinyala Canyon, 202
60-Mile Creek, 202
Skiing, 72, 127, 148, 149

admission fees to park, 7
Slide presentations, 20, 23, 114
Snack shops. *See* Dining
Snakes, 38, 40-41, 44, 45, 124, 131
Snow and snowstorms, 8, 9, 16, 88, 118
Snowmobiles, 149
Snowshoeing, 72, 127, 148
Sockdolager Rapids, 202
South Kaibab Trail, 21, 76, 86, 135, 137
South Kaibab Trailhead, 75
    elevation, 28
South Rim
    activities and events, 70-71, 80, 82-83, 84-85, 106, 114, 126-27, 144, 148
    attractions, 20-21
    best times to visit, 8, 86, 118
    campgrounds and camping, 108-109
    crowds, avoiding, 86
    dining, 99-100
    elevations, 8, 16, 28, 121
    entrance, 4-5
    future plans, 151
    hikes and hiking, 133, 135, 137
    lodging, 90-92
    maps, 13, 22, 25, 62-63, 74
    native peoples, 57-58
    nighttime, 34
    plants, 49-54, 119
    services, 11-12, 18, 210-12
    sunrise/sunset, 35
    transportation, 4-5, 6, 12, 21, 22, 73, 75, 76
    visitor/information centers, 20, 23, 80
    weather, 8, 16, 28, 88, 118, 209
    wildlife, 38, 39, 40
    See also specific activities, hikes,

· Acknowledgments ·

"It seems a gigantic statement even for nature to make."
—John Muir, in *Steep Trails*

We are indebted to Jack O'Brien and Josh Englander for their invaluable help in developing and editing the manuscript; Research Librarian Sara T. Stebbins, Museum Curator Carolyn Richard and Archivist Colleen Hyde at Grand Canyon National Park for their generous assistance with photo research and resource materials; Pam Frazier and the staff of the Grand Canyon Association for their help in locating resource materials; Tom and Mona Mesereau at Amfac Parks & Resorts and David Whiteside and the Grand Canyon Trust for their help with research; Mary Delle Gunn at the Grand Canyon National Park Foundation; and the National Park Service staff at Grand Canyon, especially Jan Balsom, Nancy Brian, Raquel Gallardo, Allyson Mathis, Marker Marshall, Maureen Oltrogge, Sandra Perl, Ellen Seeley, Laura Douris, Stew Fritts, Lynn Picard, Mike Hoffman, Bryan Wisher, and Jim Tuck for their help in making this guidebook as accurate as possible. Thanks also to Janet Dean and Pam McCosker for their invaluable help in researching, editing, and assembling the information.

About the Author

Susan Frank spent many of her childhood weekends camping in the Sierra Nevada and fishing California rivers and lakes with her family. She saw her first grizzly bear on the Katmai Peninsula in Alaska at age ten and spent more enjoyable hours waiting for fish to bite her line than actually catching them. After earning a degree in European history from the University of California, Berkeley, she taught in Minnesota and California before starting a career in communications. In 1990 she founded a media and marketing consulting company, working with a variety of clients throughout the San Francisco Bay Area.

About the Illustrator

Cartoonist Phil Frank's daily cartoon strip, "Farley," has been keeping a finger on the pulse of the San Francisco Bay Area for more than ten years, ever since Phil decided to leave national syndication to focus his considerable talents on issues closer to home. The strip is dearly loved and followed daily by a local cadre of fans. Indeed, "Farley" has become one of San Francisco's most recognized and reliable landmarks.

Susan and Phil started their life together on a houseboat in Sausalito, California. This led to their first book collaboration, a children's book about living on the water. Both avid history buffs, they moved from ship to shore about ten years ago. At present they maintain a 1914 Craftsman-style home in Sausalito, from which they venture into the national parks and other wilderness areas in search of inspiration for new books. They have two grown children, two grandchildren, two Maltese-cross dogs, and two cats.